PAMPERED
PEACE
PILGRIM

PAMPERED PEACE PILGRIM

(Finding Inner Peace While Owning Who You Are)

JENNIFER HOERL

ACKNOWLEDGEMENTS

PEACE PILGRIM – A GREAT TEACHER THAT I want to thank for showing up in my life with her messages that guided me to my goal of peace. I hope to honor her by sharing her truths, and now mine, through this book.

I want to thank my good friend Tina. We have shared so many good times and so much laughter. My journey has been truly blessed because of your friendship!

I also want to thank my friend and fellow Pampered Peace Pilgrim, Linda Parker. I love you so much! You didn't just believe in my vision, but you embraced it wholeheartedly and made it feel as natural as breathing. We are the Pampered Peace Pilgrim Partnership!

I want to thank Friends of Peace Pilgrim. Portions quoted from their book *Peace Pilgrim Her Life and Work in Her Own Words* (Hardcover Edition. Spring 1991), were instrumental in telling my story. In the copyright section of their book, they provide the following gracious permission:

"People working for peace, spiritual development, and the growth of human awareness throughout the world have our willing permission to reproduce material from this book."

I would like to extend this same permission for all material in my book.

I want to thank the Foundation for Inner Peace and the Foundation for A Course in Miracles.

Portions quoted from A Course in Miracles are from the Second and Third Editions, 1992 and 2007, respectively, published by the Foundation for Inner Peace, PO Box 598, Mill Valley, CA USA 94942.

A Course in Miracles* and the Course* are registered service marks and trademarks of the Foundation for Inner Peace.

CONTENTS

Introduction · ix

Chapter 1   The Pampered Peace Pilgrim Journey Defined · · · · · · · 1

Chapter 2   Hero – Me · · · · · · · · · · · · · · · · · 3

Chapter 3   Call to Adventure – Deep Desire For Something More · 9

     Travel · 9

     City Meandering · · · · · · · · · · · · · · · · · ·12

     Pampered ·15

     The Most Significant Trips from My Journey · · · · · · · · ·19

     Minimalism · · · · · · · · · · · · · · · · · ·24

     Buddhism · · · · · · · · · · · · · · · · · ·30

Chapter 4   Teachers · · · · · · · · · · · · · · · · · · ·39

     Peace Pilgrim · · · · · · · · · · · · · · · · ·39

     A Course In Miracles · · · · · · · · · · · · · · 44

     So Many Other Teachers · · · · · · · · · · · · · ·56

     Bono/U2 · · · · · · · · · · · · · · · · · ·56

     More Teachers To Share · · · · · · · · · · · · · ·61

Chapter 5   Setbacks · · · · · · · · · · · · · · · · · ·69

     Lack of Money · · · · · · · · · · · · · · · · ·70

     Physical Body · · · · · · · · · · · · · · · · ·72

     Judgment · · · · · · · · · · · · · · · · · ·75

Chapter 6 Goal ·81
Chapter 7 Hero becomes Teacher · · · · · · · · · · · · · · · · ·87
     Lessons From A College Professor and Others
     I Met Along the Way · · · · · · · · · · · · · · · · · · ·95
CONCLUSION ·109
MORE TO SHARE (Other Peace Pilgrims Showing Up on My Path) 113
YOUR JOURNEY ·129
APPENDIX: "STEPS TOWARD INNER PEACE" · · · · · · · · ·137
SUMMARY ·153
THOUGHTS ·157
FROM MY CORRESPONDENCE · · · · · · · · · · · · · · · · · ·163
PEACE PILGRIM'S PROGRESS · · · · · · · · · · · · · · · · · · ·169
REFERENCES ·179

INTRODUCTION

To me, peace means having no worries, fears, doubt, and especially no guilt - what I like to call true forgiveness. We all want peace, and the only thing we need to do to have peace is to just realize it is already ours. Once this understanding is acknowledged, the only outcome is the extension of peace to everyone, and we become the healers of the world. Easy, right?

To start, I don't want to claim that I am completely at peace, as that would be impossible since I am a human on the planet Earth. But I can honestly say that I have found a much higher level of peace as I have moved along this life. I also cannot offer the reader peace, because as I mentioned, they already have peace within, so they need to find their own. All I want to do, then, is to offer my journey and all of its' lessons as an example to hopefully guide the reader to their inner peace.

"The purpose of your learning is to enable you to bring the quiet with you and to heal distress and turmoil. This is not done by avoiding them and seeking a haven of isolation for yourself. You will yet learn that peace is part of you and requires only that you be there to embrace any situation in which you

are. And finally, you will learn that there is no limit to where you are, so that your peace is everywhere, as you are." (P.5: Review 1 – Workbook of a Course in Miracles)

The above quote is from A Course in Miracles, a book I will explain in much more detail later, but I think it creates the perfect mindset to begin my discussion on Peace Pilgrim, an incredible teacher, because this book is about how I want to be Peace Pilgrim…but Pampered!

I feel my purpose is to bring Peace Pilgrim's message to everyone and have them aspire to find their own inner peace, which will, in turn, bring peace to the entire world.

Chapter One

THE PAMPERED PEACE PILGRIM JOURNEY DEFINED

ELIZABETH GILBERT, AUTHOR OF *EAT, PRAY, LOVE,* and an out-standing teacher for me, once discussed Joseph Campbell's Heroes Journey. He says it is a call to adventure that is initially denied until a teacher is met; setbacks are encountered; a goal is obtained, and the hero becomes the teacher. This journey is true for each of us, and in using this formula, my journey looks like the following:

Hero – Me

Call to adventure – Deep desire for something more

Teacher – Peace Pilgrim, and many others

Setbacks - Denial – Guilt – Creation of obstacles

Goal – Find peace - Become Peace Pilgrim, but Pampered

Hero becomes Teacher – Obtained by passing lessons along – this book!

Now that I have shared the framework for my journey, let me give you a general idea of what being a Pampered Peace Pilgrim looks like for me.

In my life's journey, I feel my purpose is to be truly helpful to everyone I meet. That means accepting them for who they are and supporting them in whatever way they think is needed, without any judgement. This is what I want for myself, so I feel to receive acceptance, I must give the same. I also want to be pampered along my journey - to not necessarily have luxurious surroundings (although that would be nice) but to be treated with kindness and care. Also, because I truly appreciate when others are helpful to me, as I move along, I want to be especially generous to those who assist me, monetarily when I have extra money, but always with my own kindness and generosity.

So, my life is a pilgrimage to know peace, share that peace with others, and be pampered at the same time, so I am owning my goal of being Pampered Peace Pilgrim!

Chapter Two

HERO – ME

MERRIAM-WEBSTER'S DEFINITION OF A HERO IS "A person who is admired for great or brave acts or fine qualities.: a person who is greatly admired." To be honest, based on this definition; I truly don't see myself as a "hero" or in any of the ways depicted on TV, in movies, the news, or books. However, I am the hero in my own journey, as everyone is on their chosen roads. I don't think my story is any more important than others, but to give the reader a better understanding of my path, I will provide a brief update.

To start, I want to say that I have had a pretty blessed life and have experienced a great deal of happiness, but I have also experienced feelings of inadequacy, peer pressure – the feeling of never having the right clothes or enough money for the things I needed (wanted) to be like everyone else.

I started out in public school for kindergarten and 1st grade, and then I attended a Catholic school for grades 2nd through 8th. I remember going to church and learning of Jesus' sacrifice for my shame. We had a sacrament called Penance, where you had to sit with a priest and confess your sins. I didn't think I did anything wrong, so I would have to come up with something, and I usually mentioned being disrespectful of my parents, even though that rarely happened. I may have been mad with them sometimes, so I thought I could use that as a sin. Talk about Catholic guilt; I was creating sins that never occurred and feeling that I needed to repent for every bad thought I had. I was letting the outside world tell me I was bad or had done something wrong. I was so young – what sins could I have – I didn't get it, and I had no idea of how to apply it to my life. I could never be as good as Jesus, and I certainly couldn't die on a cross and suffer the brutality he endured to get to heaven. What hope was there for me?

We mostly covered the Old Testament in church and school, so I usually only saw the suffering that was necessary to achieve freedom. I watched The Ten Commandments every year and thought we had to go through plaques, hardships, and death to reach a promised land in 40 years- Yikes!

I felt guilty and judged all the time during that period of my life – it just didn't feel right. I couldn't let go of the shame I had developed. I tried to follow all the rules – church on Sunday, good grades, obey my parents and elders. I was a good person that never felt good enough, and I was being told I was a sinner.

I took all my grade school lessons to a public high school in the city, thinking I would leave the guilt behind me. Then I encountered not feeling adequate, peer pressure – never having the right clothes or enough money for the things I needed (wanted) to be like everyone else.

I was from a middle-class family growing up in the suburbs of a large city. I had everything I needed – I just didn't realize it at the time. So, the beginning of my "worldly/external" journey was of always wanting more and never feeling satisfied, no matter how much I achieved.

Even though I finished high school close to the top of my class, I started college, not really knowing what I wanted to do with my life. I started with Computer Science because I thought that was the career of the future and would pay off quickly. After several semesters of being miserable because I just didn't enjoy anything about computer languages, I tried other classes like Sign Language and Economics. Finally, I thought I would use my love of math to see what Accounting was all about.

All I knew was that I wanted to make a lot of money so that I could have everything I thought I wanted – nice clothes, cars, trips to wherever, whenever. I always felt like I wanted more, but I never knew what more meant. I always thought I was missing something, but never stopped long enough to ask myself what that something was, because I was always going to the next thing, parties with friends, the mall (spending money I didn't have), taking trips to places I couldn't afford – always feeling these things would fulfill me.

I had many friends and hung out with several guys until I met someone that I thought I loved. It seemed like he was just like me – wanting all the same things I wanted, so we shopped – a lot! This is when my debt started, along with the constant worry that I would never pay it off and never have everything that I wanted. I went from working at Pizza Shack, where I was paid in cash, to Payless ShoeSource to Price Club (currently Costco), where I spent 10 years of my life, because they paid well, and they kept my debt at a manageable level, while I took trips, and went to school not sure of what I wanted to do. While I was having fun, I was struggling internally, never really satisfied and wondering why. I thought I was pursuing all my dreams - funny! FYI – "funny" is a word I use often, now I see how appropriate it is to describe my life, and now I just laugh, because this worldly life is just funny.

So, I knew this guy wasn't right for me, all the signs were there, but I kept telling myself I loved him and our life together; he would change into what I needed; all of the things I knew were not true, but made me feel like I was living my dream – if only I knew what my goal actually was – I really had no clue. I always felt like I wanted more, but I never knew what that more meant.

After several years, I finally had a degree in Business Management with an Accounting emphasis, so it was time for a real career, one with fancy titles, a good salary, and some credibility to my existence. I ended up leaving Price Club – got a "real" job with the National Science Foundation as an Auditor for the Office of the Inspector General – sounds impressive, doesn't it? From there I did a lateral career move to the National Credit Union Administration as an Examiner, and I was pretty good at it, so one of the credit unions I examined asked me to be their Controller – ooh, a better title, which soon led to me becoming a

CFO – wow, my friends seemed impressed. I played it down, but I was kind of impressed too.

Soon after getting the job with the credit union, I parted ways with the guy I had thought I loved and became the independent person I knew I could be, and life was good. I bought my own house, had no debt, and thought I would be happy for the rest of my life – wrong! I still wasn't satisfied, and I didn't really know why…again. While all of these experiences that advanced me on my worldly journey made me feel like I was happy, I was never really satisfied, because I was afraid. I didn't know of what at the time, but I knew something wasn't right, and I also felt I was on a course of some sort, and I was finally starting to see God as part of it.

I now know that my internal spiritual desire that I was writing about often in my journal manifested into the worldly obstacles that kept me from feeling free because they were weighing on my soul somehow.

In general, my obstacles were some form of anxiety that can be summarized as a lack of self-confidence– the feelings of not being enough; having enough, and something is missing or could be better. For me, I was always worried about what others thought of me. I would feel lazy if I wasn't doing enough or bad if I didn't follow society's expectations, or I felt selfish if I wasn't doing enough for others.

This pattern continued most of my life, and in some respects, it still does when I take my thoughts off my goal of peace. In the meantime, I will continue my "hero" story further in the sections to follow, so the reader understands my path that led me to peace and happiness.

Chapter Three

CALL TO ADVENTURE – DEEP DESIRE FOR SOMETHING MORE

Now for the fun part of my "story," where I will talk about some of the moments in my life that demonstrated my deep desire for something more – "my call to adventure." I have always had moments where I could feel I was being guided somehow like something was pulling me in the right direction, because I had such a deep feeling of excitement about "something." However, I was frustrated because I didn't know what that "something" was or what I was supposed to do with this exciting energy. There was one calling, however, that left no doubt in my mind what I should do, and it was in the form of this deep desire to travel.

TRAVEL

I LOVE to travel! At first, I thought this passion was because I like to visit other places and that was true, but then I realized it was more about stepping outside of my box. I love exploring new places, sitting with others, who I thought were completely different from me, but ending up connecting with them based on everything we have in common.

Throughout my life, I had always wanted to travel, and I took many vacations with friends and family in my early years. But at some point, I wanted to see what it was like to travel on my own, to depend only on myself and step out of my box, so I took a leap of faith, and I went to Paris by myself, and I have been traveling on my own ever since. I took "some" French in high school, so I could speak and read very little in French, which only added to my sense of adventure. Figuring out how to navigate my way around the city, either by foot or metro, was always exciting, and I didn't mind getting lost sometimes because I usually found something interesting along the way that I wasn't expecting. I loved the challenge of making my way through the day on my own, meeting every seeming problem head-on and coming out on the other side feeling more confident in myself.

I love the total sense of freedom I experience when I travel alone. Relying only on myself and not having to coordinate with others' plans allows me to go where I want and spend as much time as I like, usually with no real agenda. Many of my friends and family couldn't understand this decision, so the first question everyone asked would be, "who are you going with?" They couldn't understand why I wanted to go by myself, and it was difficult for me to explain how much I enjoyed the time alone and the feeling of peace I encountered. I was trying something new, confronting fears and learning more about my real self with each trip. I do not doubt that these physical journeys increasingly moved me along my spiritual path.

Most of my trips fall into two categories – city meandering and pampered (this word became a part of my everyday vocabulary, thus the title of the book). I was never really into exercise but I love to walk, so city meandering involved me leaving the hotel early in the morning and just walking around the city with no real idea of where I was headed, seeing what I was meant to see, eating different foods I came upon, sitting and watching the world around me with my journal by my side. I met so many people and received so much insight about the world and myself during these trips. I would then return to the hotel each night exhausted but full of peace, which lingered after a calm bath and good night's sleep in a soft, comfortable bed.

Pampered trips are just that – a beach, mountains, any beautiful natural setting…again with my journal and books by my side. It is a bonus when I can afford spas, massages, and some of the other luxuries that come with hotel living.

I keep a journal that I use every day, and when I travel, I document every peaceful moment – every time I see or experience kindness, feel totally relaxed and free of stress and worry, or have the awareness to just breathe. Below are various trips and some of the moments or messages (in *italics*), that demonstrate how I knew my journey was leading me on my path to Pampered Peace Pilgrim. I would suggest any of my havens below to my fellow peace pilgrims.

CITY MEANDERING

Nice, France

It is impossible for me to go to Nice and not experience total beauty and relaxation. Its Cote d'Azur is magnificent, and there are so many nooks and crannies to find that offer a respite from life. It could be an open church that welcomes me to a calm space to breathe and meditate, a seat along the beach that overlooks the beautiful blue-green coast, or any one of the many cafés where sitting and journaling is a must.

Another day with endless possibilities. Before starting my journey, I am at Café Au Long Cours for my pain chocolate and tea. This café overlooks the market place with its fresh fruits, vegetables, flowers, spices, etc. The smells are incredible, and there are so many people checking out all the yummy or beautiful items. The sun is shining on my face. I feel like writing a poem.

THE CAFÉ AND THE MARKET - JENN

At a corner café
Overlooking the market
So many sights and smells and sounds
Locals and tourists
All scrambling for produce, flowers, and spices
Others, like me, just taking the beauty in
People of all backgrounds, some with their pets
Getting along
I sit here in peace.

As I wandered around, I found a church with an open door welcoming me in with open arms. I see a crucifix and am reminded of God's gift to the world – His Grace.

The children seem so happy – no cares – no concerns – can I get back to that place in my life?

Chapelle Ste. Rappaporte – My church was open, so I am sitting here now. I think I'll talk to God for a while before dinner.

Found another church – Sainte Rita – man cleaning the wood, and the smell made me smile. Others joining me as I sit – just like on the beach – unity.

The sky and the water are truly magnificent. The view of old and new Nice to either side of me is incredible. See what happens when I let God lead my steps. I need to do this more often in all my daily journeys.

Reading in the café, the rain is hitting the awning, and people are starting to seek refuge at my café. Like me, they are looking for a dry place to relax and have a meal or drink.

Finally experiencing the "torrential" downpours they were calling for, I am warm, well-fed and still have ½ bottle of wine to finish – feeling very pampered.

Looking forward to getting back to see what is ahead for me. Hoping for a move to New York and think that will happen, so I am excited, but want to remember to stay in God's hands and let Him lead me where I need to go – I think that's the best plan I can have forever – stay in the moment (always) – that's where I find peace.

New York

I have visited NYC many times and ended up moving there twice, and I will probably move back soon. It is one of my favorite cities. "Direct My Steps" was a frequent entry in my journal after I moved to NYC, and as to turn my path over to whatever higher power directing me. Below is just one of my many journal entries from my time living in the city, but I think it sums up the peace I felt wherever I went, no matter the part of the city.

> *I walked around the Reservoir many times. My first Spring in New York, I saw the best real estate in the city – a small bird's nest on a branch over the water in Central Park. It made me smile, and I looked for it every time I passed by – I am sure a sweet family lived there.*

Paris, France

My other favorite city! I felt like I belonged there for some reason, and I still do. I feel there is a calling for me to France, maybe after I retire. I think that path started for me when I decided to take French in high school. Of Course, I didn't see it then, but it was a start to a passion for Paris, and it served as more proof that I was being guided.

Some journal entries from my many trips to Paris include:

> *I am sitting in Notre Dame, an incredible place, with my friends from all over the world. I want them all to feel the peace that I feel at this*

moment - we are all free, with no guilt, fear, or lack. There is no judgment of anyone, no past to worry about and no future to be anxious about — just now.

Took the metro to Montmartre. I am sitting in Sacre Coeur again — felt like I needed it, and I wasn't here long before I started to cry. I am not sure why, but through those tears, I asked for help to get rid of negative feelings about all of the things that truly should not matter — money, weight, work anxiety.

Later - I feel like some weight has been lifted. Help me to remember this moment, and please let everyone know the peace that I feel now.

I feel much better — I will go to Sacre Coeur again tomorrow!

A woman asked me to walk her across the street. As she grabbed my arm, I noticed her hands were very soft. It was nice to feel connected to someone for a moment — I like helping others and want it to happen naturally like that more often.

PAMPERED

Tucson, Arizona

I think my first real experience of being totally pampered began when on her show, Oprah talked about Miraval Spa and Resort Life in Balance in Arizona. I had to go see it for myself, and I was not disappointed. Below are just a few of the journal entries that demonstrated the continuous peace I experienced and wanted to maintain for the rest of my life.

As we entered, we were told the "i" in Miraval means "I" – the only thing to think about. If we don't take care of ourselves, we can't do anything for anyone else.

Laying out by the pool was very calming, relaxing, and I even saw humming birds. I want to eat healthily, drink plenty of water, get moderate exercise, and just relax.

Horseback Riding – Copper – very sweet. A long ride – very beautiful scenery – very peaceful.

Life in Balance – I hope to maintain a balanced life, wherever that leads.

Sacred Springs Retreat - California

For some reason, at a point in my life I felt like I needed to be quiet. I wanted to find calm, peace and stillness, so I could see how those would feel. I wasn't sure if it was possible for me, as I was used to living in a city, being active, and having noise around me most of the time. I had read about silent retreats, and at that time, I thought it sounded interesting enough to give it a try, so I googled options and found Sacred Springs, and the peace I found is in the name.

When I arrived, I was supposed to join a group, and activities were scheduled, such as yoga, meditation, and nature walks. But, through some type of scheduling glitch (or maybe the Universe), the group couldn't make it, and it ended up just being myself, and I had full access to everything at my leisure, and I felt very spoiled. The family who ran the retreat was amazingly kind and treated me with such generosity. I was able to spend a great deal of time alone just to reflect and be quiet. I have never felt so calm in all my life, as the below journal entries exemplify.

Walking in the airport on my way to my own personal retreat, I had a good feeling that everything was and will always be good — I won't worry anymore about weight, health, or money. I just knew it would all be OK.

It's beautiful here!

Reading The Untethered Soul *about keeping the heart open. Whenever I am anxious, upset, not happy, etc., I need to realize they are past hurts, pain, guilt, and let them pass, so I don't expend any unnecessary energy. Spiritually acknowledge and move on.*

I am feeling abundant and hope this continues.

My belly is full of good, healthy things, and I am getting tired. I think I'll sleep well here with the sound of the water. The bed looks comfy!

Just Be…

- *Open to all possibilities*
- *Quiet*
- *Still*
- *A channel for nature and God to flow through me*
- *Confident in Who I Am and what I can be and have*
- *Healed*

When I think of these things, I am happy…

- *Getting rid of things*
- *Having nice things*
- *Dinner/wine with friends*
- *Being able to tip well for services I receive — massage therapists, those who help me in my travels — I think this is the purpose of me becoming a Pampered Peace Pilgrim*
- *Not working — not being around gossip, negative talk that I judge*
- *Being natural*
- *No worries about eating or spending*

Saw a hummingbird

Heard the creek

Smelled various flowers

Felt happy and content with nature.

So quiet and peaceful

I want to be happy now and then go from that point, knowing I'll always be happy. I have no problems.

The Raj Fairfield, Iowa

Several years ago, I started doing Transcendental Meditation (TM), and the Raj is an Ayurveda Health Center in Maharishi Vedic City that promotes TM. The peacefulness was palpable

– there are no words to describe the calm and restfulness that was felt upon arrival and throughout my entire stay!

I am Giddy

A white, warm, welcoming bed and lovely room

Nothing to do – no expectations

Letting fears go - unstuck – Now, all is perfect, and I trust myself that all will be OK.

THE MOST SIGNIFICANT TRIPS FROM MY JOURNEY

Honolulu, Hawaii

I went to Hawaii for the final night of U2's Vertigo Tour. Two significant events happened with this trip.

First, I think this was where my idea of being a Pampered Peace Pilgrim started. Oprah did a show around that time where she gave people $100 to pass along to someone else, and this inspired me to do the same. I gave a woman, who made and sold these beautiful ornaments, a lot more than she was asking for, and she was so grateful. I will never forget her for how she touched my life. The feeling of doing something that was so small for me, but so big for her, gave me the most sense of peace I have ever experienced. I have helped others many times, but this connection was more powerful for some reason. It's as if my purpose became clear at that moment. It gave me such a sense of peace, and I wanted to feel this way all the time. I decided that not only did I want to be pampered, but I also wanted to be generous to those that help me because I am genuinely grateful when anyone does something that makes me feel either noticed or accepted.

Second, before leaving for this trip, I wasn't feeling content with my job at the credit union where I was the CFO. I had a feeling I should be doing something more meaningful, although I didn't know what that really meant. That undefined excitement was back.

I had admired Jane Goodall most of my life. I shared her love of animals, and I gloriously found out that her foundation was not far from where I lived, so I volunteered there and was able to meet her. It was a blessing of a lifetime, as I found her to be a kind, calm and thoughtful person – it was like a divine spiritual connection. That experience helped me decide to leave the credit union and look for a job with a nonprofit, thinking that would make me feel more fulfilled. I warily turned in my notice, and although I was nervous about not having another job lined up at the time, I knew somehow it would all work out – my faith kicked in.

I had always been a U2 fan, and I saw Bono's organization, DATA (Debt Aids Trade Africa, and now The ONE Campaign), needed a Finance Director. I applied for the position, and even though it took a while, I got the job! At the final U2 show of the Vertigo Tour in Hawaii, I remember seeing DATA in the back of a program, and I just knew the job was mine. That was in December, and I started at DATA in May. I knew something was guiding me there.

My journal entries include:

Mahalo=thank you

Concert day!

U2 —everything I could imagine

Started with City of Blinding Lights, did Elevation, Vertigo — the place was moving — so powerful.

Ended singing "All I Want Is You" after playing with Pearl Jam — Rocking in a Free World - and Billy Joe from Green Day — The Saints are Coming

It was an awesome show — I am so happy to have been there to see the final Vertigo performance.

Watched sunset — found peace

I had a nice time — I really enjoyed the concert — U2 are so awesome. I am hoping I'll find a new job soon, and I am feeling confident in my decision — the more I get away and have time to think about things, the more I know I am doing the right thing.

La Paz & Oruro - Bolivia

I sponsored a little girl, Jacqueline, in Bolivia through Save the Children, and I was fortunate enough to go there to meet her. Jacqueline has grown up, so I could no longer have her as my sponsor child, but I have always supported Save the Children, and in turn, many other kids. If you feel the same compulsion about supporting children, then Save the Children is a very worthy organization.

More examples of how my Pampered Peace Pilgrim idea came to fruition follow:

Met Juan (driver provided by Save The Children) — very nice — glad I had a ride, and he was so friendly.

La Paz is in a deep valley — mountains surround — very beautiful!

Visited Jacqueline's school — met her classmates, another Juan (adorable), Tatiana, Brian — toured school with teacher and principal — they broke the current strike to come for me — feeling very special.

Jacqueline and her family showed up — made me a purse and cake — I felt like a rock star, but they are the incredible ones — mom (Nancy) has cancer, brother working in sewers, and going to school to help mother and grandmother. Jacqueline helps mother sweep streets and loves school.

Able to leave a donation for a bookshelf and some books. They called it a "library." I hope to do more of this going forward.

Kids were cute — they asked me how to say, "Thanks for coming" and "Friend" — I can't explain how incredible I felt from this connection.

Accra, Ghana & Lagos, Nigeria

As an employee at ONE, I was able to travel to Africa — I never in my wildest dreams thought I would ever be able to go to Africa, but there I was! We were there to see how communities were benefitting from the funds we had advocated for. There were so many inspirational stories, and I thought this would be a trip where I would feel sorry for others or feel guilty for what I had, but I just ended up feeling blessed for each experience.

I wanted to take each moment as it came and not think about the past or too far into the future. I also wanted to give everyone my full attention, because I really believed that was the best gift possible.

African Regent Hotel — very nice — modern — waiting to feel like I am in Africa — can't believe I feel pampered here too.

Met Ademola — happy to have gutter improvements — a mother of 2 children — girl 7 and boy 5 — living space was the size of an average US bathroom. Able to leave a contribution for rent for a larger place — felt good to help but want to do more - beautiful woman with a beautiful heart — gave me a hug — felt a connection!

Feet in the water in the Atlantic Ocean off the African coast. Will spend the day on the beach — relaxing and reflecting on the trip.

MINIMALISM

Travel showed me that I wanted to be untethered. I liked moving around with just the bare necessities, and the physical travel demonstrated my need for freedom. Once I realized this, I applied it to my overall life, which has led to a minimalist lifestyle.

As I noted previously, I always wanted stuff. I wanted to be like everyone and have what everyone had or what I thought I should have to feel accepted. I shopped often and accumulated a lot of debt for things I didn't need, and then I worried about being in debt. I always wanted more, and I felt less important when I couldn't have it all. It was a vicious cycle, and I was never pleased because I was wasting a lot of energy buying and maintaining things.

After many years and a great deal of self-help, I started realizing I was good enough, and I didn't need to prove anything to others. Taking accountability, I knew it wasn't what others thought of me, but what I thought of myself. This realization didn't happen overnight, but I eventually and gradually started feeling like I wanted to downsize. I was living in a three-level, furnished town house, and I decided to move to a one-bedroom apartment. I often moved after that—six times in nine years—downsizing each time. I am currently living in a small one-bedroom apartment, and I could only be happier if it were a studio. With each move, the only stress I had was packing my things, so I kept trying to get rid of anything that was not being used. This process allowed me to be able to move from Chicago to New York with everything I owned in a rented sedan.

It took some time to get to this point, but it was a natural progression. I want to be clear, though, that while I did downsize, and I didn't want a lot, I still wanted what I had to be nice, and I always wanted to feel pampered. This means a soft, comfortable bed with cozy blankets and pillows, clean and tidy surroundings and all aspects of my apartment in good repair. I like luxury, and I am so glad I am becoming less materialistic, always trying to downsize and simplify my life. I don't need a lot, so now I just want to be comfortable with no worries about the future.

Everyone should do what makes them happy in life. For me, I needed to get rid of stuff so that I could focus on what was more important and allowed me to find peace. At first, I thought I was lazy, and that I didn't want things, because I didn't want to take care of them. While there is some truth to this, in reality, I just didn't want to be tethered, and I learned this through my journey.

Below are some other thoughts from journal entries I recorded along the way that pointed to my minimalist path.

> *When you don't have anything to lose, there is no grief — nothing to worry about — no fear.*

> *Eckhart Tolle says if I am not looking to find myself in things, the attachment will drop away, so I am willing to give this a try.*

> *Tao Verse 81 emphasizes living without accumulating, and this verse strongly suggested replacing the accumulation of more stuff with celebrating my true essence.*

Sam Hamill wrote the following:

> *"The sage does not hoard,*
> *And thereby bestows.*
> *The more he lives for others,*
> *The greater his life.*
> *The more he gives to others,*
> *The greater his abundance."*

Below are a few Peace Pilgrim quotes from the book containing her writings. Each one reflected my journey on the minimalist path perfectly.

> *"She gradually and methodically adopted a life of voluntary simplicity. She began what was to be a fifteen-year period of preparation, not knowing just what it was she was preparing for."*

This is similar to the unknown excitement I always felt pulling me even when I didn't know where.

> *"During this 'preparation period'…she found inner peace – and her calling."*

Me too, and graciously I found Peace Pilgrim during my preparation period, and she continues to guide me.

> *"I was trained to be generous and unselfish and at the same time, trained to believe that if I wanted to be successful, I must get out there and grab more than my share of this world's good. These conflicting philosophies which I had gathered from my childhood environment,*

confused me for some time. But eventually, I uprooted this false training."

Similar to me, as I was very materialistic and thought things made me happy. It took me a long time to figure out this wasn't the case and to know that my happiness could only be found on the inside.

> *"I thought it would entail a great many hardships, but I was quite wrong. Instead of hardships, I found a wonderful sense of peace and joy and a conviction that unnecessary possessions are only unnecessary burdens."*

> *"There is great freedom in the simplicity of living..."*

> *"Anything that you cannot relinquish when it has outlived its usefulness possesses you..."*

> *"We must be able to appreciate and enjoy the places where we tarry and yet pass on without anguish when we are called elsewhere. In our spiritual development, we are often required to pull up roots many times and to close many chapters in our lives until we are no longer attached to any material thing and can love all people without any attachment to them."*

This is my exact journey – moving often and traveling whenever possible.

"The simplification of life is one of the steps to inner peace. A persistent simplification will create inner and outer well-being that places harmony in one's life."

"Some people seem to think that my life dedicated to simplicity and service is austere and joyless, but they do not know the freedom of simplicity. I am thankful to God every moment of my life for the great riches that have been showered upon me. My life is full and good but never overcrowded. If life is overcrowded, then you are doing more than is required for you to do."

"It is those who have enough but not too much who are the happiest."

"Because of our preoccupation with materialism, we often miss the best things in life, which are free."

"Unnecessary possessions are unnecessary burdens. If you have them, you have to take care of them."

"The simplified life is a sanctified life,

Much calmer, much less strife.

Oh, what wondrous truths are unveiled —

Projects succeed which had previously failed.

Oh, how beautiful life can be,

Beautiful simplicity."

I think we can all relate to Peace's messages, but it doesn't happen overnight, and that's OK. Minimizing wasn't always easy, because I always used the justification that in the future, I might need whatever I was purging at that point. To solve this problem, I decided if I haven't used something in a while (I usually use 6 months as a gauge), its value is being wasted, and someone else may be able to use it. Downsizing has been so liberating and has led me to even more peace and freedom from the past, and now that my load has lightened, I am more excited about what the future holds.

Another teacher along my path is Mark Singer, author of **The Untethered Soul.** While he doesn't necessarily focus on getting rid of things, he does provide advice for an untethered life by eliminating fear and negativity, which helped me with my minimalist path. I suggest that anyone on a spiritual path read this book in its entirety. I have read it many times and found that the below few quotes relayed the most powerful lessons.

> *"Do not let anything that happens in life be important enough that you're willing to close your heart over it."*

> *"If you close and protect yourself, you are locking this scared, insecure person within your heart. You will never be free that way."*

> *"Fear is the cause of every problem."*

> *"The purpose of spiritual evolution is to remove the blockages that cause your fear."*

"It is actually possible to never have another problem for the rest of your life. This is because events are not problems; they're just events. Your resistance to them is what causes the problem. But, again, don't think that because you accept the reality it means you don't deal with things. You do deal with them. You just deal with them as events that are taking place on the planet Earth, and not as personal problems."

"There is no reason to be afraid of life. And the fear will fade once you understand that the only thing there is to get from life is the growth that comes from experiencing it."

BUDDHISM

I am not sure how Buddhism crossed my path, but as soon as it did, I was sure that it was another alignment with Peace Pilgrim and my journey. There is so much more to Buddhism than I could possibly provide with my limited understanding, but I will share the aspects that relate to peace for me and let the reader take it from there.

While exploring Buddhism, I learned -

- Buddha knew we will all die someday, and he felt that the only thing that will count then would be how well we have taken care of our minds.

- There are three teachings of Buddhism – self-discipline, concentration, wisdom, and six Harmonies

- giving, observance of rules, endurance, diligence, concentration, and wisdom.

- Buddha advises us to listen more and speak less. We should have a kind heart, perform kind deeds, speak kind words, and, overall, be a decent person.

- Buddhism begins with eliminating all thoughts in an attempt to obtain a pure mind.

- Emptiness – this doesn't mean a feeling of loneliness. It is feeling empty of all the negative/fear thoughts that enter our minds. I tried to imagine this often and found such profound peace. The word nirvana means "extinguishing," and once I extinguished fear from my thoughts, the joy or "nirvana" remained.

- Our overall goal should be to help people free themselves from suffering, experience peace, and realize their true nature.

- Happiness is to want what you have and not want what you don't have.

One Buddhist teaching I noted said that renunciation is the decision to give up attachment so that nothing becomes an obstacle to your spiritual progress or a waste of your time and energy. While this seemed to align with my minimalist philosophy, it really meant more. It says we don't need to give up anything really; we just need to give up the attachment we have on our things.

I realized that once I didn't have an attachment to my stuff, it became so easy to let most of it go.

Buddha considered craving and ignorance to be the root of all suffering, and he thought that severing all desires would stop all worries and troubles. Buddhist philosophy revolves around eliminating suffering, and below are some Buddhist habits that I uncovered and applied to my life. They have helped me minimize suffering and guided me to more peace.

Simplify – Buddha was born a prince, so he could have accumulated as much as he wanted. However, he knew that material things were not needed, and he understood there had to be more than just the physical. For me, minimalism just became so natural that I didn't want things anymore. Not only were they not fulfilling me, but they were also making me feel unsettled and tethered.

Meditate – Buddha says that beneath our unconscious mind is a transcendental spiritual dimension, and this is our true nature. Because I want to find my true nature, I often try to be still and quiet my mind. Please notice I said "try," as this isn't always easy for me.

I always wanted some type of meditation in my life, but I could never find a kind of practice that worked for me. I hear this often from others as well. For me, Transcendental Meditation (TM) is very effective, as it doesn't say to stop thinking, but to just be still and let thoughts come and go. Eventually, the mind will calm down. I do have this calming experience often, and I enjoy the peace that comes when I feel silence and freedom. I never thought I could do this twice a day for 20 minutes, but I found myself craving it more and more.

By being in the now and letting the past go, which meditation allows, I have such a sense of calm moving forward. Maharishi Mahesh Yogi (TM founder) says, "Life finds its purpose and fulfillment in the expansion of happiness." Meditation helps me find the happiness that is deep inside, and once I find it, I can carry it with me as I move through my day.

Follow the Wise – Learn from elders or more experienced people that come into your life. For me, actual examples of 'the wise' are Peace Pilgrim, Bono, Oprah and many more that I will discuss further under the Teachers section below.

Always be Mindful – This means no judgment or evaluation of anything or anyone, including myself.

I always thought my life should be what everybody else thought it should be, so I was always worried about what others thought of me, and in my mind, it was that I was never good enough. As I mentioned, it took a while, but through my spiritual journey, I finally realized that all the negative feelings of lack in some way were my judgments of myself. I had always thought others were judging me, but in truth, I had no idea how others felt about me, so any judgment of me was coming from me.

I was happy on the surface. I was traveling, shopping, accumulating things and showing the world, and proving to myself that my life was perfect. I was always trying to do the right thing, so people liked me, and I was being an overall good person. I thought I had a great life, but I still wasn't satisfied. I still wanted more but couldn't figure out what the real desire was inside.

Jesus was a huge part of growing up Catholic, and later in life, I was able to get past the guilt that this upbringing brought. I was then finally able to accept Jesus' message of unconditional love - there was nothing wrong with me – I was loved. Looking back, it seems like everything was aligning along my Pampered Peace Pilgrim journey, and now I am mindful of not judging myself, others, or situations.

So, after a great deal of self-help, I realized, ultimately, I just wanted to be happy. I didn't want fear in my life, so I started being mindful and looking for peace in everything, and eventually, that's what I found. I chose love and acceptance over fear. I learned that this yearning for peace inside was due to my faith and belief that I deserved happiness. It resulted in my willingness to want and expect more, and also helped me understand that I could have what I wanted without guilt, which is also true for everyone.

Working on having no judgment and letting the past go, I find I have fewer opinions, and this is a good thing because it allows me to see things from different perspectives. I think opinions can be hurtful because they create defensiveness rather than acceptance. All our stories are different, so what is right for one may not be for another, and that's OK. The Course suggests seeing things from "above the battlefield." When you pick a side, defensiveness is inevitable, but if you are above the battlefield, you can see both sides, and knowing all the facts allows for a more peaceful resolution.

"Nothing is more conducive to peace of mind than not having an opinion," says Lichtenberg. I always say, "it is what it is." My opinion doesn't change anything, and for me, it has become a fun activity to say "whatever" when events occur that I cannot control. Having an opinion doesn't change it.

Words hurt, so we really need to be mindful of what we say to each other and remember how we feel when we hear something derogatory about ourselves. We need to always be mindful to put ourselves in the other person's shoes. As an example, I really don't like the word "stupid," and I cringe every time I hear it. I genuinely believe there is no such thing as a stupid question—peace proves no one is stupid. They just don't know any better at the time, and we all need to understand that about each other and the circumstances that occur in our lives.

I should avoid taking one position and sticking to it, no matter what the circumstances are, and I should aim to be in harmony with all people, especially those whose opinions conflict with mine. I need to remember to include myself when giving kindness and ensure that I am not judging. I also need to decrease my criticism while increasing the amount of courtesy and goodness in the world. I always want to try to be mindful of complaining about anyone or anything because it only adds more drama and negative energy to a situation and solves nothing.

In general, we should always affirm that we see ourselves in others and choose to be in the space of goodness rather than judgment. I like the word "Namaste," as it means "I honor the place in you where we are all one."

Maya Angelo said, "when you know better, you do better," so by acknowledging the situation as a lesson, we know better, then we can move on to do better. I was also able to use this with my obstacle of judgment. If I am making mistakes, so is everyone else, and as such, I need to always remember this fact and offer peace rather than judgment.

Embrace change – Buddha believes everything changes – our minds, bodies, surroundings – so if we accept this premise and find peace with it, life will be much calmer. Recognizing that everything changes makes living in the past an impossibility. When we try to change the effects of the past, we are only disappointed, and this leads to the next step in Buddhism.

Live in the Moment – This means not going over the past repeatedly in our minds and no worrying about a future we have no control of the outcomes.

My favorite quote is from Lily Tomlin, who said, "Peace means giving up all hope for a better past."

A lesson I learned early in life played on an acronym for the word "bad." Often, we look back in regret at some of the "bad" decisions that we made. We go over and over in our heads what we should have, could have or would have done. We spend so much time there (and sometimes never leave) that we don't look to the future, and we lose hope. In these moments, we just need to stop and say that BAD = Best Available Data and understand, at the time, that's what we used for that decision. Then, moving forward, we just need to try to build on the current data and do better to be ahead of the game next time.

While implementing my BAD theory, whenever I thought I made a mistake, I heard someone use the same theory by saying, "acknowledge and move on." I thought it was brilliant and one of the most influential messages I had ever heard, so now I use it all of the time. It goes back to "it is what it is."

I think most of my friends want to strangle me when I give this advice – it sounds so uncaring or dismissive, especially in certain situations, but I always believe it. Even when it is hard advice to take myself, I truly believe it is what started my path to peace. It's about being in the "now" – no past to regret and an open future – how freeing is that? There isn't anything in the past that can be changed, so we need to let it go. It is best to acknowledge it, take its lesson, then move on – that is what peace is - not holding on to things that do not bring peace. These include grudges, resentments, mistakes, guilt, fear – you name it. Tell me one good thing that comes from holding onto the past?

This all seems like meaningful guidance, so I try to incorporate these lessons into my daily life, and I think they have helped to improve my level of peace. Buddha was one teacher along my path, and now, I want to share the many others that showed up to help me reach my goal. There have been so many, and I feel the primary purpose of this book is to share what I have learned from each. Therefore, the next section will be the largest, and hopefully, the most inspirational to the reader.

Chapter Four

TEACHERS

PEACE PILGRIM

SEVERAL YEARS AGO, A FRIEND SUGGESTED I read the story of Peace Pilgrim (Mildred Lisette Norman), so I found a book about her life, and it changed mine. She didn't write her story, but it was a compilation of her writings, as I feel my book is a compilation of my thoughts from my journal entries and lessons I have learned along the way. I think Peace's book was another seed planted for me, and I am sure her journey showed up in mine, so I can use it to continue her truth…and now my truth.

Portions quoted from Friends of Peace Pilgrim's book *Peace Pilgrim Her Life and Work in Her Own Words* (Hardcover Edition. Spring 1991), were instrumental in telling my story. In the copyright section of their book, they provide the following gracious permission:

"People working for peace, spiritual development, and the growth of human awareness throughout the world have our willing permission to reproduce material from this book."

It also says in the introduction to their book:

"It is our hope that her words and spirit will continue to inspire."

"We hope this book will be a valuable resource for these and future writers, as well as an inspiration and encouragement to those who never had the good fortune to meet her."

Allowing me to pass her wisdom along to others freely is such a blessing, I feel it is both an obligation and an honor to share the enlightenment I received with as many people as possible.

As I followed Peace Pilgrim, I wanted to learn as much about her as I possibly could, and I was blessed to actually meet her sister, Helene Young, who is currently 104, and one of the most amazing and kind people I have ever met. I also corresponded with the Director of Friends of Peace Pilgrim, Bruce Nichols. He connected me with Helene, and he is also one of the nicest and most helpful people I have ever known. Peace Pilgrim surrounded herself with wonderful individuals, and I hope this book introduces many more to her, and her message continues to permeate our world.

So, what is Peace's story? She was a woman who gave up all possessions (everything she owned she carried in a blue smock), and walked across the US seven times from 1953-1981 (25,000 miles until 1964) during the McCarthy era, Korean War and Vietnam War with her message of peace:

"When enough of us find inner peace, our institutions will become more peaceful, and there will be no more occasion for war."

To start, I will share some of Peace Pilgrim's many messages, followed by how her influence showed up in my life by providing highlights of my journey. I will then share similar messages from other sources that have had a huge impact on my life.

Peace – *"If you want to make peace, you must be peaceful."*

"When you approach others in judgment, they will be on the defensive. When you are able to approach them in a kindly, loving manner without judgment, they will tend to judge themselves and be transformed.

"From all things you read, and from all people you meet, take what is good and leave the rest."

"Inner peace comes through relinquishment of self-will, attachments, and negative thoughts and feelings. Inner peace comes through working for the good of all."

"There is no greater block to world peace or inner peace than fear."

"When you find peace within yourself, you become the kind of person who can live at peace with others."

I have previously discussed judgement, which directly relates to Peace's quotes above, but I had further insights as well. I was asked once what superpower I wanted. At first, I thought it was the ability to speak all languages to be able to communicate with everyone. Then I decided language wasn't enough, and it was the ability to understand everyone, seeing them for who they really were on the inside and not the drama they projected - total acceptance, love, peace, and understanding.

For me, acceptance of everyone started when I learned the Golden Rule early in my life, and it was something I always tried to apply. "Do unto others, as you would have them do unto you." I will admit, at first, I thought it was about Karma — what comes around goes around. But this understanding always seemed a little selfish to me, because I sometimes felt I was being kind for my own benefit - I had to be kind to everyone so that I could experience kindness. Regardless, I followed the rule all the time and started to learn to give everyone the benefit of the doubt, knowing there was more going on than I knew.

I focused on the way I wanted to be treated, and then I made sure I was always thoughtful when dealing with others. For example:

- I wanted to be heard, so I always tried to stay present and listened when others spoke.

- I never wanted to be embarrassed, so I tried to always be empathetic, never embarrass anyone, and accept them.

- I never wanted others to talk about me, so I tried never to say anything bad about anyone.

- I always wanted kindness shown to me, so I always tried to be kind.

- I never want to have my feelings hurt or feel judged, so I always try not to do this to others.

Early in my career, I took a diversity training course, and I learned about the Platinum Rule. Instead of "do unto others as you would have them do unto you," it became "do unto others as they would want you to do unto them" – accept them – no judgment of anything they have done, past or present, and be open to their future. Currently, I just want to be what others need me to be in their lives. I want to be understood, so I try to understand.

We all just want to be unconditionally loved and accepted for who we are—all of us, with no exception. If I can do this for everyone I meet, I feel I am fulfilling my purpose. It's not always easy because we cover up who we really are with our stories and drama, but the love is there. So, we just need to keep trying to see love and peace so that we can always offer our acceptance to everyone, all the time.

We all have different journeys in life, but the truths of Peace Pilgrim are universal and a positive way to unite us all in the common goals of love and peace.

Because of Friends of Peace Pilgrim's gracious allowance to reproduce materials, I am providing *Steps Toward Inner Peace* in its entirety in Appendix A. I feel it is so incredibly important, and I encourage the reader to take the time to read Peace's amazing guidance. Friends of Peace Pilgrim offer this as a pamphlet that can be obtained by contacting them at <u>https://www.peacepilgrim.org</u>. It is free and an excellent gift to give to anyone.

A COURSE IN MIRACLES

"The purpose of your learning is to enable you to bring the quiet with you and to heal distress and turmoil. This is not done by avoiding them and seeking a haven of isolation for yourself. You will yet learn that peace is part of you and requires only that you be there to embrace any situation in which you are. And finally, you will learn that there is no limit to where you are, so that your peace is everywhere, as you are." (P.5: Review 1 – Workbook of a Course in Miracles)

I used this quote at the very start of the book, because I think it aligns with Peace's ideals, it reflects how I want to become a teacher like Peace, and because it is from A Course in Miracles (the Course), this is a good introduction to the next huge and most impactful source in my life.

I believe in a Higher Self that I call God, Awakened, Consciousness, or Universe (for consistency, I will use God throughout the book). I grew up Catholic, so Jesus was also a big part of my life, but unfortunately, his messages of love were not the focus of my education. Attending Catholic middle school and church, we read bible passages and stories mostly from the Old Testament, and we were told what they meant and how we should apply lessons to our lives, because, as sinners, we needed this guidance.

After Catholic grade school, I attended a public high school, and I started going to church less often and pretty much stopped after meeting all of the Catholic sacrament requirements. While I liked going into churches for some of the peace they brought, I didn't get anything from the actual services anymore, because all I felt was judgement, and I couldn't reconcile this feeling with what I wanted – love and peace. I needed to be closer to God somehow, so I thought I'd try services at various churches of different denominations. I attended a Lutheran service, and before it started, as a new attendee, I was asked to stand up and introduce myself. I am not a public speaker and very introverted, so I never returned to that church. I also tried Episcopalian and Presbyterian, and for one reason or another, they just didn't feel right to me, so I kept searching.

I was blessed to eventually find and start attending Linden Linthicum United Methodist Church. This was just the start I needed to my spiritual path, as the Reverend there was another great teacher to cross my path. He didn't make me feel guilty about anything, and he actually thought I had something to contribute, so I ended up doing more for that church than I had ever wanted to do growing up Catholic. One of my favorite "jobs" was setting up the church for Sunday service. I would go in the Saturday before, when there was no one around, perform my duties and then spend some time reflecting and just soaking in the calm and peace that surrounded me. I still find joy thinking about being alone in such a quiet, peaceful place.

It was during this period in my life that I found The Course. I can't remember when or how it came into my life, but it was definitely through my yearning for peace. I had had a taste of peace, and I wanted more. The Course was a difficult concept for me to grasp at first, so I wasn't consistent in my reading, but then one day it clicked, and I couldn't put it down and had to see where it led.

I was fortunate enough to find an incredible mentor not long after I started doing the Course wholeheartedly. I met Annette Lantos through a friend, and she had been practicing the Course for many years. She is the widow of Congressman Tom Lantos, and both survived the Holocaust in Nazi-occupied Hungary. Congressman Lantos was the only Holocaust survivor to serve in Congress, and Annette is an amazing woman, friend, and teacher, so learning about peace from her was a fantastic experience, and I can never thank her enough for the lessons she provided. In fact, she is the person who introduced me to Peace Pilgrim – another reason for my gratitude.

A Course in Miracles seems like a strange title, so let me explain. It is a holy book using modern education techniques. It is not a religion – there are no buildings – no egos – just Jesus' words of love and peace. It states that "Instead of a divine interven-tion in the physical world which heals the body (ego), a 'miracle' is a divine intervention in our minds which heals our thought-patterns," and it is in our minds that true healing begins. It goes on to say "that the key to healing the human condition is within our grasp, within our own hearts and minds. In the choice to forgive, we can escape all the pain and suffering of the world, we can bring healing to the hearts of others, and we can be reunited with God."

Designed as a "Course," it has three volumes: a text, a workbook for students, and a manual for teachers. At the start, it provides 50 principles of miracles. A few that relate to my peace journey and align with Peace Pilgrim's message are as follows:

#3   Miracles occur naturally as expressions of love. The real miracle is the love that inspires them. In this sense, everything that comes from love is a miracle.

#11   Prayer is the medium of miracles. It is a means of com-munication of the created with the Creator. Through prayer, love is received, and through miracles, love is expressed.

#13   They undo the past in the present, and thus release the future.

#18   A miracle is a service. You recognize your own and your neighbor's worth simultaneously.

#21   Miracles are natural signs of peace. Through miracles, you accept God's peace by extending it to others.

#27   A miracle is a universal blessing from God through me to all my brothers. It is the privilege of the forgiven to forgive.

So, the miracle is peace – our common goal – Peace Pilgrim's philosophy! For me, peace is forgiveness - true happiness, unconditional love that we can have now – "on earth as it is in heaven." It is derived from seeing everything, every situation, and everyone, including myself, as if for the first time every time without seeing the story, the "drama"; and accepting what is going on as it is in the current moment. It is definitely what I want, because it brings freedom from the past, freedom from guilt and suffering, freedom from fear. It is Peace, Love, Light, Happiness, and Home. I believe we are all united in this desire, and we all want these things in our life. If I want if for myself and others, and I offer it to myself and others, how better would the world be?

The Course often refers to the "body," and it includes the ego, physical body, and emotions. It is an unconscious dream world created by us. It is the body that needs to be corrected through peace, and this correction occurs by undoing our ego story of fear and guilt and finding peace and happiness. The Course uses the lower case "self" when referring to the body. The upper case is used when referring to the Spiritual, Enlightened, Awakened "Self."

Below is my own very brief summary of The Course's premise of our origin story:

1 - We are one with God – our Higher <u>S</u>elf

2 - We had what the Course calls "a tiny mad idea" to separate from God. We should have laughed at this idea and returned to God, but instead, we thought we left Him.

3- Because we thought we left, we became guilty and afraid that God would punish us, so **we** took that guilt and fear, and **we** created a second world of an ego-<u>s</u>elf, that is just a dream or illusion where **we** believe in sin and are never satisfied or happy. We want to go home – wake up – but we have so much guilt and fear that we don't know how to get back. The Course notes:

> "Yet the Bible says that a deep sleep fell upon Adam, and nowhere is there reference to his waking up. The world has not yet experienced any comprehensive re-awaking or rebirth. Such a rebirth is impossible as long as you continue to project or miscreate. It still remains within you, however, to extend as God extended His Spirit to you. In reality, this is your only choice because your free will was given you for your joy in creating the perfect."

So, the good news is we never left God; we just **think** we left Him so that we can return to Him at any time. God is just waiting for us to decide to wake up from our dream. He doesn't bring any suffering or even know of it – He only knows love, which is within us, as the Holy Spirit, who is the gift God gave us to help us get back to love.

How freeing is that – the choice is ours, so we can live in fear and guilt, or we can choose love and return to God.

Following this premise, the Course says that there is one problem and one solution for **anything** that doesn't give us peace. The problem, as stated above, is we think we have sinned, and we are separate from God. The solution is there is no sin because we are not truly separate from God - He never left us. When we thought we separated, He gave us the Holy Spirit and Jesus to guide us back to Him. They are using the dream we have created here on Earth to undo our fear, erase our story. If we let go, sur-render, we will have more clarity of our Higher Self and decide to go home. Sin actually means "to miss the mark," so we are only mistaken in the dream. We just need to give our journeys to the Holy Spirit; be patient; and let things happen as they will, knowing all will be OK and anything is possible with God's love.

I knew about the Holy Spirit, but in church it was called the Holy Ghost, so I really didn't understand when or how He was helping me. In looking for peace, the Holy Spirit became my true friend. I was always talking to Him – asking for help, ranting about my doubts and fears - and I realized He was using every situation to help me undo my story, and all I had to do was go along for the ride, knowing He wasn't judging me; loving me unconditionally; and using everything I experienced as a guide home. I love hav-ing this relationship, so I try to be that friend to everyone I meet, and it always brings me peace. So, my goal is peace for everyone, including myself, and I am willing to give my journey to the Higher Self. I went from focusing on the Crucifixion (guilt and judgment) to focusing more on the Resurrection (new life and joy) and Jesus' teaching of no fear and only love.

The Course helped me really understand what true peace meant, and it perfectly aligned with Peace Pilgrim's message, as it is all about forgiveness, which I have found to be true peace. The Course has been in my life for so long now, it has become engrained in my being, and there is so much to share, but I will highlight only some of its aspects, messages, and guidance below that I think are either helpful or peace-related.

The Course is a course in mind training that teaches us to make the choices that will heal inner conflict and bring inner peace instead. It says we must work on a deep inner malady - not an unfair conflict between ourselves and outside forces, but a conflict in our own mind, between our freely chosen beliefs and our best interests. This is similar to modern psychology, which asserts all human ills are rooted in mental illness, so all solutions lye in mental healing.

The "Miracles" in A Course In Miracles is forgiveness. It is the main theme that runs throughout, and for me, it can be substituted for peace. It says for every problem, there must be a better way, and that way is found in forgiveness.

The Dalai Lama has said, "my religion is kindness," and I feel this aligns with The Course's main message of forgiveness of self and others. It is not a religion that is sectarian in its themes, but "a universal Course." It is similar to Eastern Religions – Hinduism and Buddhism, as it professes:

1. The world we live in is just a dream.

2. Reality is outside space and time, beyond comprehension as we know it – The Course calls it "Heaven," and this is who we really are.

3. The goal is to wake up, to realize who we really are, to unloose our attachments to this world, and awaken into unlimited bliss.

The Course calls a "holy instant," that moment we lay aside our characteristic patterns of thinking and feeling, which have failed us, and open ourselves to receive the truth, to receive "a better way."

The Course has some similarities with traditional Christianity. But Christianity says the root cause of our predicament is embodied in the idea of sin and salvation as our way out. The Course, however, implies that by labelling sin and evil, and time and space real, Christianity have subtly added to our burden of guilt, reinforced our limitations and made God a punisher, instead of one of love. As I mentioned earlier, this is how I felt growing up Catholic.

The Course seeks to correct this perception through purification. It says the key to our release is the fact that both our condition and its cornerstone, sin, are somehow dreams, and "only what God wills is real, and God wills only limitless love." However, The Course does not aim at teaching the meaning of love, for that is beyond what can be taught. It does aim, however, at removing the blocks to the awareness of love's presence.

By emphasizing peace instead of love, the Course says the problem of sin must be undone before the goal of love can be achieved. No matter how much energy we pour into trying to love others and ourselves, we will never succeed until we erase from our vision the dark cloud of sin, and this is done with forgiveness and peace.

Heaven = "pure oneness – no bodies, no different places, and no separate moments of time. There is only an infinite expanse of unified awareness," "…the experience of perfect boundless love, a joyous union with all that is."

We feel trapped between Heaven and the world, and every impasse in life is this one. We all want something better, we want to be happy, but we seem to be trapped by forces beyond our control, but the Course says the world cannot trap us, limit us or control us, for the world is an illusion. Heaven is the only reality. Our true nature has never left Heaven, and is there this very moment, completely unaware of the world. Heaven is now and will always be our home. We need only awaken to where we are. Our goal, then, is not to change ourselves, or even to 'grow,' it is merely to change our thinking and wake up to the unlimited, innocent Son of God that we already are.

Letting go of the world seems to be a horrifying leap into noth-ingness, and we cannot make it alone, so God gave us the Holy Spirit to bridge the gap – we just need a "little willingness." He realizes we cannot awaken from the world instantly, so He leads us home gradually.

We don't need to overlook the world, but simply to see it differ-ently. Bodies (objects and events), being illusions, are entirely neutral. It is our own perception, our own interpretation of them that gives rise to our experience of life. And this perception is an internal matter. It is our own free choice. The ego-self is just a deeply ingrained belief that we are separate. We seek to be what The Course calls "special" or unique, so we try to conquer the world around us.

We relate to the world either by –

- attack – see sin in others to bring love to us – "It is the judgment of one mind by another as unworthy of love and deserving of punishment." This leaves us feeling guilty and alone, so we seek allies by…

- "bargaining" or "giving to get"

Both have the same purpose of bringing into our lives what the Course calls "idols" – money, possessions, achievements, abili-ties, and beauty, etc., which seem to be the purpose of life. This produces quilt, and we think if we sin, we deserve to be pun-ished, which leads to self-loathing.

The ego feels supported and strengthened by guilt, and we have no alternative but to hide from guilt, and we use the below defense mechanisms –

- Denial, which hides guilt inside and finds its way to the subconscious. Projection, which reinterprets our guilt, telling us that what seems to be our guilt is actually someone else's.

- We blame others to escape blaming ourselves.

As we know, this only makes us feel fearful all the time because we are always accusing ourselves and others of sin, and the ego's end result is fear, isolation, guilt, and loneliness.

The Course says the ego is not what we are – we are not sinful or separate – we are still as God created us: forgiveness, love, and peace. It doesn't matter how bad we think we are, we really just want love, but it is in the form of self-worth that we seek to be loved by others and ourselves. What looks like sin is really just a call for love.

Steps to forgive others –

1. Identify the problem – take a clear, honest look at what we think of others – search for any unloving thoughts.

2. Let go of the problem – realize there is **no true reason** to hang onto hate, express it, or support it.

When we empty our minds of all the darkness, we wipe the slate clean.

3. Healing – allow God to transform our minds and infuse us with the gift of love. The effects of healing do not stop with the other, but all minds are joined, so any act of peace impacts the entire universe.

To sum up the Course - by simply changing our minds, by forgiving, we come to see a part of Heaven in everyone and everything we look upon. This is Peace Pilgrim's goal, now my goal, and I hope everyone's goal eventually.

SO MANY OTHER TEACHERS

Peace Pilgrim and The Course were the biggest influences on my spiritual life, and there were many others put on my path that offered similar messages to only reinforce my desire for peace. Each guided me in some form or another, so I will share their inspiration next.

BONO/U2

From a music perspective, U2 has probably had the most influential impact on my life. At the time they came into my world, I wasn't sure why I needed them, but I obviously did, because 30+ years later, their music, and especially Bono's lyrics give me such peace.

My U2 experience started when I was in college. A friend of mine invited me to their concert in D.C., and even though I didn't know anything about the band or their music, I decided to go along. I rarely attend concerts unless I know the words to every song an artist performs, so seeing U2 was a rare occasion for me, but it ended up changing my life. It was like going to church, but better.

After an amazing performance, the band ended with the song 40, which truly moved me and still does to this day. At the time, I didn't realize it was the psalm. It was the last song on the album "War," and the band ended their concerts with this beautiful prayer during the Joshua Tree tour. 50,000 people left that show singing together a psalm of belief and hope, and the refrain borrowed from Psalm 6 - "How Long To Sing This Song?," which was a cry in the opening line to the band's other popular song Sunday Bloody Sunday, about the death and violence experienced in Dublin, but it was speaking to me spiritually as a plea for how long I would experience my life as an ego rather than the Higher Self I truly am. It also gave me a sense of unity with others, because as one, we continued singing, "I will sing, sing a new song," as we left the concert, walked to the metro, and even still on the metro ride home – we all shared the same promise of hope. This concert was so powerful for me because so many were joined in truth, and this gave me an internal sense of belonging and even more faith in God.

U2's lyrics are very similar to the words to Psalm 40 found in King James Version (KJV) of the Bible -

I waited patiently for the Lord, And He inclined unto me and heard my cry.

He brought me up also out of a horrible pit, out of the miry clay, and set my feet upon a rock and established my goings.

And He hath put a new song in my mouth, even praise unto our God; many shall see it and shall trust in the Lord.

These words continue to give me hope and strength through God's love for me. They were the start of my U2 obsession, and I began to listen to all of their music, as well as learn everything I could about the band.

I learned their Christian beliefs are demonstrated in the words to all of their songs, and most contain at least one verse from the scriptures. Many songs could be interpreted as written about romantic love, but I always found them referring to God, and they were probably the most subtle but powerful influence on my spiritual journey.

Bono, the lead singer and writer of most of the band's lyrics, said, "The soul will be described, but God might not use the people that you expect." For me, He used an Irish rock band to help me hear His words, and I am glad they shared their songs, messages, understanding, and guidance. I loved all of their songs for the music, but it was Bono's words that were the most inspirational. They reflected peace, love, and forgiveness when I really didn't know what any of this meant. They resounded in a way that moved me, and I didn't know why.

I have been blessed to work for Bono's organization, ONE, an international advocacy campaign to end extreme poverty. I was able to meet him on a few occasions and can honestly say he is a kind and thoughtful person. I could feel the sense of peace he radiated – a fellow peace pilgrim (and he would admit pretty pampered also).

One of the highlights of my obsession with U2 was when the reverend of the Methodist church I mentioned earlier encouraged me to give a U2 service - WOW! Talking about U2 and God, I was blown away. As I mentioned, I am not a public speaker, and usually, the thought of speaking to a group terrifies me, but I was so excited when the Reverend first mentioned a service with U2's songs, mostly because I knew I was being directed by God, and He was with me. I was sharing something that has meant so much to me and my spiritual life, and I knew my truths would resonate with others, and they would find the same closeness to God that I had felt.

My "sermon" was really just me introducing three U2 songs along with their videos. The first song I shared was one that many were probably familiar with - *I Still Haven't Found What I'm Looking For.* The band was actually criticized for this song, because if they were Christians, how could they not have found what they were looking for in Jesus. However, Bono describes the song as "a gospel song for a restless spirit," very similar to a psalm, and the words clearly state the band's true beliefs when Bono states that Jesus "broke the bonds," "loosed the chains," and "carried the cross and my shame."

I think Bono felt that following Jesus is a journey, not an arrival. This implies that action is required, and we need to walk the walk. For Bono, and many, it is wanting the world to be a better place to live. This is his and my belief that the cross can and should be making a difference. That difference is what we are looking for. Bono has tried to reach that goal with his work in Africa, trying to relieve the debt and fight aids and poverty through his ONE campaign. He feels AIDS is the leprosy of today, and it can't be ignored.

Another line in the song says, "I have spoken with the tongue of angels." This comes from 1 Corinthians 13:1, which says, "if I speak in the tongues of men and of angels, but have not love, I am only a resounding gong or a clanging cymbal." Love is what the band, and all of us, will continue to keep looking for and hopefully find when we reach out to those in need and do the Lord's work.

The next song I chose was *Yahweh*, and it is the last song on the album, *How to Dismantle an Atomic Bomb* and drives home its main theme of surrender. This song is about giving over to God to sort out our life and ask God to take all that we have and use it for the betterment of the world. The song concludes with the words, "take this heart and make it break."

Bono has said in many of the band's songs that a heart that hurts is a heart that feels, and by feeling and having compassion for others' pain and suffering, we can try to be and do better.

Immediately following Yahweh, was the song 40, which I previously discussed. Everyone seemed responsive to my message, and several people approached me afterwards, because they were also U2 fans, and felt the same as I did about the band's messages. I was so thankful to them for letting me share something that has meant so much to me and my spiritual life. It was one of the first times I had a sense of certainty in myself and my message.

MORE TEACHERS TO SHARE

Oprah

Oprah came into my life when I was in high school. I lived in Baltimore when she started doing the local news. I remember the ads asking, "What's an Oprah?" so I tuned in, and I liked her personality. After she moved to Chicago, I didn't follow her much until she started her "change your life" shows, which did change my life, and I still follow her on *Super Soul Sunday*.

A funny side note – I attended one of her shows in Chicago, and the topic was "Inside the Taliban," which was relevant at the time, but I was a little disappointed (I was really hoping for her giveaway show). However, I was able to shake her hand and see that she didn't just talk the talk, but she walked the walked, as she was very approachable and kind to everyone, and this was something I wanted for myself, so I was appreciative of her example. Besides appearing to be a kind and caring person, she surrounds herself and shares with everyone, other impactful individuals that try to heal our world with profound insight. She is probably the original Pampered Peace Pilgrim who inspired me, and I can't thank her enough.

Below are some of the more relevant influences on my peace pilgrimage. I have included only small samples of their works – the information I feel is most worthy. I suggest reading all of these books in their entirety for the inspirational detail they provide.

The Four Agreements – written by Miguel Ruiz – probably the most readily understood and easy to apply book that kept me moving on my peace journey because the agreements were the answers to all of my obstacles.

I did an exercise once that revealed the self-limiting, fear-based beliefs that made me unhappy. They included –

- I am not good enough
- I'll make a mistake
- I'll be wrong
- I'll be judged
- I'll look bad
- People will make fun of me
- I won't have enough
- I'll be unhealthy – suffer an illness
- I'll say the wrong thing
- I'll hurt someone's feelings – upset others, and they won't like me

Any of these sound familiar?

Miguel Ruiz showed me that I need to break these "ego agreements" and replace them with the Four Agreements below to become stronger.

1. Don't take anything personal – probably the most difficult. I used this whenever I felt any type of confrontation. I would try to see it from the other person's point of view, and I tried to tell myself it was their fears motivating them, so I shouldn't take it personally. Easier said than done!

2. Don't make any assumptions – in every situation, we don't know all that's going on, so we should always try to give everything and everyone the benefit of the doubt

3. Be impeccable with my word – this isn't just about always telling the truth to others, although that is important, and I have always tried to never lie. This agreement was more about what we tell ourselves in every situation and being honest with our intentions. The words we use about ourselves create the energy that surrounds us, so it is always best to be loving and kind to ourselves and others.

4. Always **try** to do my best – all we can do is try. We don't need to beat ourselves up for making mistakes, as long as we try to do what is right and in our and others' best interests. BAD (Best Available Data) had started this process for me.

Each of these agreements has become a guiding force for me.

Elizabeth Gilbert

Elizabeth Gilbert's book, *Eat Pray Love* so inspired me, I decided to follow her lead and take a year off to write my first book. I met her in Chicago at a book signing event, and when I thanked her for her inspiration, she stopped, took my hand, looked me in my eyes and thanked me. I admired her ability to make each person feel special, so that has become a goal of mine as well.

In her book, among much guidance, she provided the following questions to ask:

In the morning, as you wake up, ask, "What do I really, really, really want?"

My answer was easy - peace in every situation.

In the evening, as you fall asleep, ask, "What made me happy today?"

> My answers are always a list of the things that have to do with peaceful interactions with others, whenever I was helping someone along our mutual paths, and when I found quiet peace within myself.

These helped me remember to always touch base with my Higher Self in order to align with my peace journey, and then be grateful at the end of the day for what I accomplished.

Gary Zukav

When I first saw Gary Zukav on an episode of The Oprah Show, I must admit I didn't entirely get his message, but something must have stuck in the back of my head because I always felt compelled to watch any show he appeared on. I finally decided to pick up his book, *Seat of the Soul,* and in it, he said intentions are the "single most powerful source," because they create the effect. That message resonated with me as another truth that would guide me on my peace path. I always want to do everything with the intention of peace.

Here are some lessons I took from Gary while watching him on Oprah, as well as from his book:

- I need to align my personality with love, clarity, understanding, and compassion to gain power.
- Authentic needs belong to the soul.
- There is no power in fear, or in any of the activities that are generated by fear.
- Humbleness, peace, clarity, and love are freedom. They are the foundations of authentic power.
- When I want something that I do not have, instead of what I do have, confront it. I should challenge it each time that it comes up by realizing that when it comes up, I am not in the present moment, and not engaged in my present energy dynamic but, rather, letting energy leak to a future that does not exist.
- Instead of a soul in a body, become a body in a soul. I should look for my soul. This relates to a

Course lesson that says, "I am not a body. I am free, for I am still as God created me."

Eckhart Tolle

Oprah once had a course for *A New Earth – Awakening to Your Life's Purpose* by Eckhart Tolle, so I made the commitment to take it, and it was another opportunity to connect with my Higher Self, and it really guided me to the peaceful path I desired.

Some thoughts that showed up during this course:

- If the thought of lack – about money, recognition, or love – has become part of who I think I am, I will always experience lack.
- My inner purpose is to awaken.
- Fulfilling my primary purpose is laying the foundation for a new reality, a new earth. Once that foundation is there, my external purpose becomes charged with spiritual power because my goals and intentions will be one with the universe.
- Awakened doing is the alignment of my outer purpose with my inner purpose.
- Acceptance means: For now, this is what this situation, this moment, requires me to do, so I do it willingly.
- I cannot manifest what I want; I can only manifest what I already have. I may get what I want through my efforts as the ego, but that's not real.

> Jesus said, "Whatever you ask in prayer, believe that you have received it, and it will be yours."
>
> • Jesus told his disciples, "Heaven is right here in the midst of you."

I later read Eckhart Tolle's other book - *Oneness With All Life – Inspirational Selections from A New Earth*. It beautifully summarizes the material from *A New Earth – Awakening to Your Life's Purpose* and seemed to speak directly to most of my obstacles.

More thoughts that showed up from Eckhart Tolle:

- I have access to God through the present moment, so if I turn away from it, God won't be a reality in my life.
- Attachment to things drops away by itself when I no longer seek to find myself in them.
- I need to give up defining myself to myself or to others. I shouldn't be concerned with how others define me. When they define me, they are limiting themselves, and it's their problem for not seeing the entire picture. Whenever I interact with others, I shouldn't be there as a function or a role, but as a "field of conscious Presence."
- I don't become good by trying to be good, but by finding the goodness that is already within me and allowing that goodness to emerge.
- Don't seek the truth. Just cease to cherish opinions.

All of the other teachers (other heroes) I shared above have such similar messages that seem like universal truths, so I wanted to give them the credit they deserve. They have led the way, so by sharing them with the reader, I am showing my gratitude. I am so thankful for their guidance, and since I received, I want to give back.

Chapter Five

SETBACKS

Setbacks for me are anything that causes fear and takes away my peace. I think my obstacles are similar, if not the same, as everyone's obstacles, and in general, are some form of anxiety, that for me can be summarized as a lack of self-confidence— the feelings of not being enough; having enough, or something is missing or could be better. As I noted, I always worried about what others thought of me. I would feel lazy if I wasn't doing enough, bad if I didn't follow society's expectations, or selfish if I thought I wasn't doing enough for others.

I think these are common among us all and want to share how they showed up for me, how I explored them, and, most importantly, how I have forgiven them. Through each step, they lessoned or disappeared entirely.

LACK OF MONEY

As I mentioned earlier, I always thought I needed money and things to make me feel important and to have people accept me, but it also seemed there was never enough money to accomplish this goal. When I left home, I had no savings, and for instant gratification, I would shop often and accumulate debt – buying things I didn't need and going places that were well outside of my budget. Because I didn't want anyone to know about my debt, I also always felt like I had a secret. This embarrassment was heightened by the fact that I had a business and finance background, so I wanted everyone to think I was financially strong.

I often felt like I had to work hard to support this lifestyle, so the good news is I created a great work ethic, and I have always been a valued employee that was respected for the job I performed. The bad news is that I never gave myself enough credit for this work ethic because I thought I was only working hard for the money, rather than being the hard worker I really was, and I was always afraid I may lose my job, because I didn't feel worthy.

Fortunately, on my journey, I was introduced to other teachers such as Suze Orman and Maryanne Williamson, who helped me understand the role money should play in my life. I feel everyone has trouble finding peace around money, so I just want to share some lessons I have learned along the way that have influenced my ability to find peace in this area.

Suze Orman

I read many of her books, and while she helped me get financially organized, it was her spiritual messages that had a more lasting impact. Basically, she said money doesn't make me who I am. I could find love and peace regardless of what was in my bank account.

In addition, she always ended her show by advising that we put "people first, then money, then things." This showed me that my intentions are important, so I always need to investigate what they truly are and how I can use money in the best way possible to bring me peace.

Marianne Williamson

In her book, *The Law of Divine Compensation – On Work, Money, and Miracles*, she shared that the world is an abundant place, I deserve the abundance, and if I don't think I do, it's my own fault.

This revelation came from her message that God promises me love, which doesn't come in any form, such as money. I already have God's love, so I have everything I need, and I just need to surrender my talents and ask God to use them to help heal the world.

I always felt I had to work hard to have abundance, but this thought interferes with nature's belief in abundance. Marianne says, "your job is simply to be, joyfully expressing your own inner worth-and the universe will find a way to take care of you." She goes on to say, "You are empowered not because you have money, but because with that money you can help empower others.

You're not coming from a 'get' mentality; you're only allowing the flow of universal energy to move through you and use you in a way that serves a greater good. Bless every dollar, and every dollar will then bless you."

After reading this book, my new truths became:

1. I have more than I'll ever need
2. I don't need things to make me happy.
3. I have control of my money

While I still have thoughts of lack from time to time, the lessons above remain in my consciousness. I was able to turn things around – supporting myself, having money in the bank, and having no debt. Now I want to have enough money to do only the work that makes me happy – to become Pampered Peace Pilgrim and find comfort for myself and also be able to spread the wealth. I now know I will always have enough money to support anything that brings me peace. I have everything I need, so I don't need to worry about anything, ever.

PHYSICAL BODY

My overall health has been a challenge throughout my life. When I was young, I had a heart murmur that was corrected with open heart surgery when I was thirteen. Also, at a relatively young age, I needed to have a hysterectomy, which was in conjunction with having Cushing's Syndrome, so menopause and many other unpleasant symptoms came instantly, and my body has been rebelling ever since that period of my life. This has probably been one of the biggest challenges I have had to face, and not just because of the bodily challenges, but because of the fear they create, and the feeling of my faith being tested.

While health issues were present most of my life and always created some type of fear or anxiety, I learned that God wants love and happiness for me, so I tried to figure out how I could obtain peace with regard to my body, even as I struggled daily with some bodily issue or another. I tried to focus only on peace, and I wanted to be grateful for what was going right in my life. The truth was that everything that happened to me was manageable, and there were always kind people in the medical field that helped me along the way. I am happy to say that as of right now, I am as healthy as I have ever been.

Another body anxiety had to do with weight. Most of my life, I have been pretty thin, but like everyone, I always worried about my weight, what I was eating, and how it impacted my appearance or health. This always produced more fear or anxiety, which I think is true for most people, and I also think everyone knows that overeating isn't about food, but it is about something that is going on inside. It's our thinking and worrying about it all of the time that creates fear, so if we're not thinking about it and letting it control us, it's easier to overcome.

I took a stress management class in college, and the teacher said that when you go to eat something, ask, "am I really hungry?" If not, don't eat, but do something else as a distraction. I thought this was good advice, but I needed more, and Kenneth Wapnick, a Course follower, in his book *Overeating - A Dialogue on Application of the Principles of A Course in Miracles*, provided the addition of asking your Higher Self for help in these moments. So, now if I ask, "am I really hungry?" and say "no," I step outside of my ego and ask how I should proceed and then wait for the answer. This keeps me more present with food, so I am not thinking about what I ate, or what I am going to eat, with any regret, because I am doing it with God in the moment, giving Him any fears that I have, and I am at peace.

I have also always believed that I should eat everything in moderation. So, if I am really hungry, I try to figure out what I am hungry for, and that's what I eat, whether it's a salad, pizza, or ice cream. By allowing myself to eat anything whenever I want, and trusting it's the right thing, I don't worry about food so much, and maintaining a normal weight has become much easier.

The Course has more advice on how we see the "body." It guides that the ego says, "you're empty," so we must fill up ourselves, and the ego also says, if we don't keep feeding the ego, it will die. The purpose of overeating (or any addiction) is to reinforce feelings of lack or separation. What we all yearn for or hunger for is our Higher Self. We know there's something missing. We feel unworthy of God's Love, because we believe we have separated from Him, but God's love does not depend on whether we are good or bad, thin or overweight. There is not a lack in us, so we don't need to fill it with food, and the goal should not be to lose weight but to feel better about our self and not feel guilty.

JUDGMENT

I saved the most difficult obstacle for last, because it has been the largest setback in my life, and it has always brought me fear and guilt.

In learning and understanding that I am creating my world, I discovered the concept of projection. What I see in others is what I see in myself. So, if something or someone doesn't give me peace, I need to figure out why, so I can correct it in myself. This not only helps me improve, but it makes me thankful for anything negative that shows up in my life because I know that it is there for a reason – to show me what I need to let go and forgive in myself.

I learned, and believe, that a brother, and myself, will never find peace in this lifetime if I am placing any limit on them or myself. Limits are placed when we only look at the surface story and judge it. This includes our own stories- my story is the things I tell myself about all of my obstacles.

Everyone is different on how much of their story is blocking the love in them. We need to accept everyone, knowing for them that Love is in them. I once heard, "be kind to everyone because you don't know what everyone is going through." This is good advice in any situation.

We judge based on our own stories of guilt and fear that we created, so not only should we not judge, but we can't, because we don't have all of the facts, we only have the parts of the story being projected. So, the solution is to judge as God would judge – only with love. Justice = "Just is" – no right or wrong – we don't have all of the information when we judge, so we need to allow the Holy Spirit to judge for us, which would be only from love and acceptance.

The Course showed me that I need to turn all judgment over to God – His justice is all that matters, because He is the only One that can see in totality, and His judgment will always be that of love – no one is guilty of anything! We just need to trust Him, look past our stories, and love everyone, including ourselves.

Jesus said, 'Forgive us our trespasses as we forgive those who have trespassed against us.' He understood that the first step of peace is to accept other people just as they are, even if they have harmed us."

The Course says:

> "When everyone is welcome to you as you would have yourself be welcome to your Father, you will see no guilt in you."

> "To forgive is merely to remember only the loving thoughts you gave in the past, and those that were given you. All the rest must be forgotten."

> "It is as sure that those who hold grievances will suffer guilt, as it is certain that those who forgive will find peace."

> "My grievances hide the light of the world in me."

When I hold grievances, my world just gets darker and full of more clouds, but if I can forgive, let go of all my grievances, I move toward the light, the Truth, God, and my true Self, and I take everyone with me.

Below are several Peace Pilgrim quotes and how they relate to my journey to remove judgment.

> *"My motives were pure, and much of my work did have a positive and good effect. I used what I call spiritual therapy: I found all the good things that those I worked with wanted to do, and I helped them to do those things."*

I now try to listen, accept, and support everyone on my path in the manner that they feel they need and not based on what I think they need.

> *"My approach is to help with cause rather than effect. When I help others, it is by instilling within them the inspiration to work out problems by themselves. If you feed a man a meal, you only feed him for the day – but if you teach a man to grow food, you feed him for a lifetime."*

I always use this analogy, but with fishing - if you give a man a fish, he will eat for a day, but if you teach a man to fish, he will eat for a lifetime.

> *"When angry, or afflicted with any negative emotion, take time to be alone with God. (Do not talk with people who are angry; they are irrational and cannot be reasoned with. If you or they are angry, it is*

best to leave and pray.) Visualize God's light each day and send it to someone who needs help."

So, with the Course's and Peace's advice, I tried to see everyone, including myself, as guiltless. I learned that my feelings of lack created my judgments, so with God's love now in my world, and learning there is no lack, I am able to eliminate some of these fears.

Being human, I will always judge, but now I try to see things from a different perspective. I learned that we all do things for two reasons – to find love or to remove fear. This helped me give others the benefit of the doubt. When someone is bitter or mean – it's because they are afraid or lonely, so I need to offer love and acceptance – anything else, just makes things worse.

I know we all judge everyone and everything all of the time. Judging others makes it easier to make them "wrong" and us," right." It makes the problem "outside" instead of in us. It takes away our responsibility to deal with our own stuff. I heard someone say that when we point a finger, there are three pointing back at us, and what we judge in others is really what we need to correct and forgive in ourselves, so I started asking what my judgments of myself were, and I was able to address them.

As I observed my judgments more and more, I learned that most of them occur when I am out in public, and they relate to the idea that people are thoughtless or uncaring- rude or inconsiderate. I usually judge, because others don't see me, cut me off, stop in front of me, etc. First off, I know it's not physically intentional, and I am also sure it is not spiritually intentional. It's my stuff showing up – feeling unworthy. Now I laugh at it more and let it go.

I also realized that everyone wants to be heard, seen, accepted, noticed, etc., but unfortunately, they seek these things through their "drama." They do things to be acknowledged, and it can be in a good way or a bad way, but either way, if we just accept them, it provides the love they need. If we overlook the "drama" and know they just want love, why not give it to them rather than judge them? This can be difficult, and my ego will always judge, but my spirit knows better, so I just keep trying to remember this lesson as often as I can.

I always try to overcome obstacles, and as a result, judgement has turned into new and more positive thoughts in my life that mostly can be summed up as "No Past." The Course and Peace ask that we let the past go. If we aren't dwelling on the past, we can be in the moment with our Higher Self. How many times have we been worried about something? How many of those times do we remember now? They came and went, all were resolved, so we can have faith that everything – all problems in this world will be resolved. This too shall pass; it is finished because we are eternal, and God is always working for our best interest, so we just need to remember this through every situation and listen to Him always.

The Course also says, "The miracle enables you to see your brother without his past, and so perceive him as born again. His (and my) errors are all past, and by perceiving him without them, you are releasing him." "This means that you perceive a brother only as you see him now." "His past has no reality in the present, so you cannot see it. Your past reactions to him are also not there, and if it is to them that you react, you see but an image of him that you made and cherish instead of him." "When you have learned to look on everyone with no reference at all to the past, whether his or yours as perceived it, you will be able to learn from what you see now." So currently, I try to ask, "am I a blessing to those around me, or a burden? Do I lift guilt from them, or do I lay it on them?" I am here to be a channel of God's grace to the world and to release everyone I come into contact with from their guilt, most especially from the guilt I have laid upon them.

I want to be happy, and when I am, it is more natural for me to want to bring peace to others. I now know when I find my happiness, it is extended to others naturally.

Judgment is something I always want to try to correct because I know freedom from judgment will bring me and everyone peace. While judgment will always be a part of the ego world and something I will always have to work on, I can honestly say, it is so much less evident in my world now.

Chapter Six

GOAL

So, I HAVE DISCUSSED WHO I AM, the many teachers that have guided me, and the setbacks in my life. All of these have led me to my goal, which I think is pretty obvious, but let me just make it clear – I WANT TO BE PAMPERED PEACE PILGRIM (thus the title of the book).

Peace Pilgrim said - "It is my mission as a pilgrim to act as a messenger expressing spiritual truths. It is a task which I accept joyfully, and I desire nothing in return, neither praise or glory, nor the glitter of silver and gold. I simply rejoice to be able to follow the whispering of a Higher Will."

She also defined a peace pilgrim in the following quote –

"What do peace pilgrims do?" *"A peace pilgrim prays and works for peace within and without. A peace pilgrim accepts the way of love as the way of peace, and to depart from the way of love is to depart from the way of a peace pilgrim. A peace pilgrim obeys God's laws*

and seeks God's guidance for one's life by being receptively silent. A peace pilgrim faces life squarely, solves its problems, and delves beneath its surface to discover its verities and realities. A peace pilgrim seeks not a multiplicity of material things, but a simplification of material well-being, with need level as the ultimate goal. A peace pilgrim purifies the bodily temple, the thoughts, the desires, the motives. A peace pilgrim relinquishes as quickly as possible self-will, the feeling of separateness, all attachments, all negative feelings."

Like Peace, I also want to be a messenger…but with a twist. I was and still am inspire by Peace Pilgrim, and I believe all she believes, but I want to be pampered, that's who I am, so I am owning Pampered Peace Pilgrim. I decided to take all of Peace's wisdom and apply it to my life. I want to be the messenger of her incredible words, as well as those of other great influencers I am sharing in this book. I want the reader to take these insightful messages along their paths to own and enhance their journeys.

At first, I admired Peace's ability to give up worldly possessions, but I thought that type of sacrifice would be impossible for me. Initially, I felt guilty that I didn't share her willpower to give up everything and to be able to live the simplest life possible. Peace slept wherever she stopped, or wherever she was invited to sleep, and she ate only when given food. In the beginning, I knew this wasn't a lifestyle that I aspired to, because I had so much stuff that I "needed." But then I realized that was Peace's journey, and I have my own journey. Everyone's path is different, but the goal is the same – peace and happiness, and as I noted, I am closer to becoming a minimalist, and I am always looking for ways to downsize. This outcome was definitely inspired by Peace Pilgrim.

Another area where I seemed to differ from Peace Pilgrim was in my difficulty to deal with big-picture aspects. That seems overwhelming, and I felt I was too small or unworthy of being able to impact change. With time and guidance, I changed my perspective and accepted that I was more into the details, so I started there in dealing with one person at a time, and this worked for me. Peace showed me that world peace must start with inner peace, so I am working at the ground level first with myself, then I can expand to those I meet along the way.

While we differed in stories, it seemed many of Peace's messages were mine as well, and I felt such a connection. I believe that we are all one, so when I am peaceful, others feel my peace, and it is extended. This is my spiritual pilgrimage.

At some point along my path, I realized I had always been a pampered peace pilgrim, so I just chose to claim it. I knew it was what God wanted because I felt peace with that thought. Once again, I felt my worldly journey was being used for my spiritual journey, and the introduction of the Course enhanced this belief. As noted above, the Course has been another major influence in my life, and I feel one of the purposes of this book is to relay its message as well as Peace.

The Course says, "Humility will never ask that you remain content with littleness. But it does require that you be not content with less than greatness that comes not of you." It goes on to say,

"You have the right to all the universe; to perfect peace, complete deliverance from all effects of sin, and to the life eternal, joyous and complete in every way, as God appointed for His Holy Son."

I believe this truth because I know God wants me to know his abundant love and peace, so I can strive for more and more with no guilt, because it all comes from my faith.

I felt like Peace, and the Course was guiding my spiritual journey toward happiness, but for my worldly journey to align, being pampered would be required. I wanted to experience luxury along the way. I wanted to be the Peace Pilgrim that stayed at the Westin. I am a member of Bonvoy (a Westin/Marriott hotel chain), and they just happen to have a Heavenly Bed collection, which fits right in with my pampered criteria.

My current pilgrimage to peace is writing this book, while still enjoying any luxuries that are important to me like the following:

- Feel peaceful, happy, content, interacting with others without feeling distracted with guilt, worry or fear related to other worldly things (job, money, etc.)

- Feeling limitless

- Always being present with everyone I meet - try to be a good listener.

- Spreading wealth where it is needed – to people who need the most appreciation.

- Having leisure time to volunteer more. When I lived in NYC, I volunteered through New York Cares', and my favorite project was helping kids with their homework after school, and I loved it – it brought such peace and happiness. I want this to be my job.

- Traveling wherever and whenever

- Visiting Spas as often as possible – I always find peace from the smells that calm as soon as I enter a spa.

- Massages – why go to a spa, if I don't want to find total relaxation

- New, clean, fresh surroundings always

I wanted to keep my idea of becoming Pampered Peace Pilgrim to myself, as I didn't think anyone would really understand this goal – it seemed odd enough to keep to myself. Then one day, for some unknown reason, I hesitantly shared it with a friend, and I was blessed to have her not only accept me for this seemingly crazy idea, but she also felt the same way. What are the odds? After that moment, the energy created whenever we come together to discuss this idea is palpable. I am always giddy before, during, and after our get together, and this feeling has propelled us along our path. While we discussed it often as a fun idea, on August 11, 2016, my great friend, Linda, and I officially started the Pampered Peace Pilgrim Partnership as we spoiled ourselves with breakfast at Edgar's, a very upscale, posh restaurant in the Mayflower Hotel in Washington, D.C.

I thought formalizing a plan would represent our intention to put it into the universe in hopes that one day, it would become our reality. The Partnership was based on Linda and I coming into a large sum of money (we never wanted to say an exact amount, because we were open to as much as would be provided), so that we could pamper ourselves, as well as share with those that crossed our path. The plan was that whenever we traveled, we would tip well to everyone that helped us, including transportation workers, masseuses, manicurists/pedicurists, hotel employees, and waiters/waitresses, to name a few.

The other aspect of the plan is that our "jobs" would be to meet regularly (at a pampered place) on determined intervals to discuss how we can anonymously help people we have met who may need a little kindness.

Our motto is - **Be Happy To Make Others Happy!** We believe this strongly aligns with Peace Pilgrim's theory, so we think it is a solid mission statement.

We are still waiting for the large sum of money, but just thinking about our plan, makes us so happy. It is always fun to talk about it, and we are able to implement the plan on a small scale each time we meet by tipping well when we can and making as many people as possible happy along the way. I am confident this plan will only expand until we have reached the Pampered Peace Pilgrim Partnership full potential.

Chapter Seven

HERO BECOMES TEACHER

YOU MAY HAVE NOTICED THAT THE GOAL section above was not very long, because I genuinely believe it is not about the goal as much as it is about the journey, and the major part of my journey is to be a teacher.

The Course's Manual for Teachers states the following –

"A teacher of God is anyone who chooses to be one. His qualifications consist solely in this; somehow, somewhere he has made a deliberate choice in which he did not see his interests as apart from someone else's. Once he has done that, his road is established, and his direction is sure. A light has entered the darkness. It may be a single light, but that is enough. He has entered an agreement with God even if he does not yet believe in Him. He has become a bringer of salvation. He has become a teacher of God."

"They come from all over the world. They come from all religions and from no religion. They are the ones who have answered. The Call is

universal. It goes on all the time everywhere. It calls for teachers to speak for It and redeem the world. Many hear it, but few will answer. Yet it is all a matter of time. Everyone will answer in the end, but the end can be a long, long way off. It is because of this that the plan of the teachers was established. Their function is to save time. Each one begins as a single light, but with the Call at its center, it is a light that cannot be limited. And each one saves a thousand years as the world judges it. To the Call Itself has no meaning."

"There is a Course for every teacher of God. The form of the Course varies greatly. So do the particular teaching aids involved. But the content of the Course never changes. Its central theme is always, 'God's Son is guiltless, and in his innocence is his salvation.' It can be taught by actions or thoughts; in words or soundlessly; in any language or in no language, in any place or time or manner. It does not matter who the teacher was before he heard the Call. He has become a savior by his answering. He has seen someone as himself. He has therefore found his own salvation and the salvation of the world. In his rebirth is the world reborn."

Lesson 20 says, "I would behold the proof that what has been done through me has enabled love to replace fear, laughter to replace tears, and abundance to replace loss. I would look upon the real world, and let it teach me that my will and the Will of God are one."

I feel inspired by all these messages, as they emphasize my path. I always felt a calling of some kind, and I so want to be a teacher of peace. The Course also says, "I am here only to be truly helpful. I am here to represent Him Who sent me. I do not have to worry about what to say or what to do, because He Who sent me will direct me. I am content to be wherever He wishes, knowing He goes there with me. I will be healed as I let Him teach me to heal." I just need to surrender to a higher self and know I am being guided.

I am the middle child, and because of the gaps in our ages, my siblings and I were always at different places at different times in our lives, and we were always doing our own thing. I don't see this as good or bad, really, but I do think it was used to define part of my story.

The "good" that came from this is the independence that I felt as part of my path. Also, I thought I received attention by trying not to stand out, so I think this helped me learn humility early on in my life.

I found an article about middle children on Facebook many years ago, and it demonstrates how even though I wasn't aware at the time, my path was leading me to the same understanding as Peace Pilgrim and the Course.

Some highlights from the article regarding middle children follow -

- Middle children are often overlooked. It's usually not intentional, it's just that the older sibling blazes the trail for us, and the younger sibling is the perpetual adorable baby, so our job is just to fit in.

- Although it can be frustrating to have to fight harder for their parents' attention, there are specific benefits of being a middle child. They are peacemakers because they can see both sides of any argument, and always try to find the "win-win."

- As children, before bullying the younger sibling, they naturally stopped to think about how it felt when they were the victim. On the other hand, they also gained a better understanding of respecting their older sibling's privacy, because they knew what it was like when their annoying younger sibling invaded their room. As a result, they are very empathetic, and they were born for a mediating or consulting job, and people probably seek them out for advice. People may think they have no preference, but really, they're just flexible, and they understand that the majority vote wins.

I was so amazed when I saw this article because it basically defined my childhood as a middle child, and it proved I had been on the right path all along, and I could own my desire to be a peace maker.

Like everyone, I have always been a pilgrim – going through my story. I want to continue to share the lessons I have learned and become the teacher that I know I can be. I have started already by sharing some of Peace Pilgrim's, the Course's, and others' messages in the Teacher section of this book. Below, I will continue to be imparting more understanding I have acquired from those listed above, as well as some new wisdom. My goal is to be a good teacher to the reader, so they may pass along what they feel is relevant to them in order to demonstrate their own teaching abilities.

More passages, as well as some of Peace's quotes from the book *Peace Pilgrim Her Life and Work in Her Own Words* follow. All of these quotes align with my life in some form or another, as I will explain under several of the messages. I truly believe everyone can use them on their journey.

"When you know your part in the scheme of things, in the Divine Plan, there is never a feeling of inadequacy. You are always given the resources for any situation, any obstacle. There is no strain; there is always security."

Once I knew my goal, I found a peace that allowed me to move forward without guilt or fear. I had so much more confidence in myself that it didn't matter what others thought. I just moved forward, knowing I was being guided by something bigger than me.

"...results should never be sought or desired. Know that every right thing you do- every good word you say — every positive thought you think — has a good effect."

This was difficult for me because I was results orientated and I wanted instant gratification, so if I didn't see the good right away, I would lose faith. But I finally understood if

I just did everything with God, it was all good, no matter how it seemed to my ego, so I followed this advice from Peace -

"All I did was to surrender my will to God's will. My entire life has prepared me for this undertaking. This is my calling. This is my vocation. This is what I must be doing. I could not be happy doing anything else."

"'I never want people to remember me except in connection with peace,' she said. To those of us who knew her well and saw her over a number of years, she will always remain the serene, warm-hearted Peace pilgrim – full of humor, vitality, and the joy of living."

This is how I would love to be remembered – this is the life I want to live!

"'The seeds of peace have been scattered well. It is the duty of all who were touched by her to begin the harvest.'"

This is my purpose and the main reason for writing this book.

"You know the power of thought. You're constantly creating through thought. And you attract to you whatever you fear."

This is the reason I try to remove fear from my life whenever possible. I only want to attract what is good.

"Concealed in every new situation we face is a spiritual lesson to be learned and a spiritual blessing for us if we learn that lesson. It is good to be tested. We grow and learn through passing tests. I look upon all my tests as good experiences. Before I was tested, I believed I would act in a loving or non-fearing way. After I was tested, I knew! Every test turned out to be an uplifting experience. And it is not important that the outcome be according to our wishes."

"If you have a long face and a chip on your shoulder, if you are not radiant with joy and friendliness, if you are not filled to overflowing with love and goodwill for all beings and all creatures and all creation, one thing is certain: you do not know God!"

"Also, life is like a mirror. Smile at it, and it smiles back at you. I just put a big smile on my face, and everyone smiles back."

"We people of the world need to find ways to get to know one another — for then we will recognize that our likeness is so much greater than our differences, however great our differences may seem. Every cell, every human being, is of equal importance and has work to do in this world."

EVERYONE!!!

"If you're worrying, you're either agonizing over the past which you should have forgotten long ago. Or else you're apprehensive over the future which hasn't even come yet. We tend to skim right over the present moment, which is the only moment God gives any of us to live. If you don't live the present moment, you never get around to living at all.

And if you do live the present moment, you tend not to worry. For me, every moment is a new and wonderful opportunity to be of service."

"If you realized how powerful your thoughts are, you would never think a defeatist or negative thought. Since we create through thought, we need to concentrate very strongly on positive thoughts. If you think you can't do something, you can't. But if you think you can, you may be surprised to discover that you can. It is important that our thoughts be constantly for the best that could happen in a situation — for the good things we would like to see happen."

"Every time you meet a person, think of some encouraging thing to say — a kind word, a helpful suggestion, an expression of admiration. Never think of any right effort as being fruitless. All right effort bears fruit, whether we see the results or not."

"To know God is to reflect love toward all people and all creations. To know God is to feel peace within — a calmness, a serenity, an unshakeableness which enables you to face any situation. To know God is to be so filled with joy that it bubbles over and goes forth to bless the world."

This reflects how I feel about being a Pampered Peace Pilgrim. I never thought I could feel giddy about anything, but I can honestly say, I cannot stop smiling when the thought crosses my mind.

"Whenever you bring harmony into any unpeaceful situation, you contribute to the cause of peace."

"Yes, all human beings have a calling, which is revealed to them through an awakening of their God-centered nature."

"I learned that I shouldn't be pushy about helping, but just willing. Often, I could give a helping hand – or perhaps a loving smile or a word of cheer. I learned it is through giving that we receive the worthwhile things of life."

I totally agree with this advice. I don't want things pushed on to me, so I make sure not to do the same to others. We all just want acceptance, so I start there, and if anyone wants my opinion, I wait for them to ask.

"Live the present. Do the things you know need to be done. Do all the good you can each day. The future will unfold."

This is the best advice I could take and give to anyone. This quote hangs above my desk at work and guides me through my day to day life.

LESSONS FROM A COLLEGE PROFESSOR AND OTHERS I MET ALONG THE WAY

Early in college, I took a stress management class, which is somewhat comical considering I didn't really know what stress was at the time. Regardless, I had an amazing teacher who taught me incredible lessons early on my path. One of which was the B.A.D. theory I mentioned earlier. This and other lessons were true blessings and more evidence of life giving me teachers to guide me on my peace pilgrim journey. I hope the reader finds similar encouragement.

Accountability

One of the most significant messages I learned in that class said that people and things don't upset me, I **let** people and things upset me. This was a huge revelation for me for two reasons – 1) it brought the issue inside where I could deal with it internally with my higher Self, and 2) it gave **me** control over every situation because I was accountable for what I was thinking. Now, as inspiring as that sounds, I didn't always use it and would still blame the world from time to time for my problems (and to be honest, I still do sometimes), but it was a good building block, and the more I used it, the more I remembered its strength, and I can truly say so much less bothers me these days, because I don't let it!

People In Our Lives

Some other valuable advice that was provided had to do with relationships. The teacher said, "you can't change someone, and if you think you can, you're only fooling yourself." While I knew this, it didn't stop me from staying connected with individuals that only added drama to my life because I wanted what I thought was better for them, and I thought I could help in some way. With this lesson, though, I realized I can't push someone to change if they are not ready, and all I could do is wish them peace and recognize that if having them in my life didn't give me peace, it was better to let them go.

Now, I try to never change anyone! This philosophy did help to get me through breakups with minimal heartache, and I can happily say I am still friends with all my past relationships. There are a few friendships that are still a little challenging, mostly because I still see them struggling, and I really want to help, but I am always able to hold my tongue. I want to be accepted for who I am, so I make sure I offer the same courtesy to others. I also make sure I don't have any guilt about not keeping people in my life. I once heard that people come into our lives for a reason, a season, or a lifetime, so once I determine where someone fits in my life, I give only the necessary energy to maintain the relationship that allows for peace with no guilt.

Laughter

My father said I should be a comedian, and I thought **that** was funny, and I had no clue what he meant. I could never stand up in front of people, but I do think I have a bit of a sense of humor, and I love to laugh. I love stand-up comedians, comedy movies, and especially sitcoms. Growing up, I liked watching reruns of *The Mary Tyler Moore Show, I Dream of Jeannie, That Girl, and I Love Lucy*, actually pretty much any comedy shows or movies. I was not a big fan of drama shows, and I never watched horror movies. That still holds true today, and what is kind of funny is that some of the sitcoms I watched when I was very young reflect how my life turned out. Looking back, I realize I sort of became these characters. I think *The Mary Tyler Moore Show* was one of my favorites, and I became an independent working person, with many fun and funny people in my life, ...and some great apartments. *That Girl* was another favorite - another independent woman living on her own in New York City – check! I also wanted to live in Jeannie's bottle. I couldn't pull off that outfit, but many of my wishes have been fulfilled, and all of my apartments were small and cozy.

While I couldn't be a comedian, I do try to use humor or laughter to make others smile to get them out of their drama or story, so they can stop taking themselves so seriously for a moment to breathe. Usually, this entails me figuring out some positive aspect to what seems so negative and try to interject it with levity. I think we all need to laugh at ourselves more often. We take ourselves and our stories way too seriously.

As mentioned earlier, the Course said we should have laughed at the "tiny mad idea" to separate from God, so I am glad I had laughter in my life early on. Peace offers more opportunities for me to laugh and be silly, sometimes even in "bad" situations. Nietzsche says, "Let us slay the spirit of gravity – not by wrath, but by laughter."

I also heard that a laugh is universal because it doesn't need translation and represents happiness. This is a form of the previously mentioned universal superpower I wanted. If we are all happy, it is much easier to communicate with and understand everyone. Ella Wheeler Wilcox said, "laugh and the world laughs with you, weep, and you weep alone."

Gratitude
Laughter and happiness are just a few things I am grateful for, and they entered my life because of my huge appreciation for gratitude. I kept a daily gratitude journal for many years, and I still make sure to remember to be thankful in some way each day.

If I have one suggestion for anyone, it is that they do the same, as it transforms your life from negative to positive, even if it is only in a small sense at first.

I started by writing five things each day. Sometimes it was the same five things from the day before, but it really did adjust my attitude. Sometimes it was me "talking the talk," when I wasn't necessarily "walking the walk" at the time, but I could feel a shift occurring, so I made it a habit.

Some of my common themes –

> *Neville and Phillip —my two cats, who brought so much joy and peace to my life. Whenever they would curl up next to me, or I watched them sleep, or when they were silly boys getting into something they shouldn't – I never got mad – just smiled. They were a definite part of my peace path.*

> *Days when I didn't have any plans*

> *Nice weather, sunshine, being with nature*

> *Finding things – books, quotes, etc. that made me feel like I was improving my life somehow.*

> *The good feelings I had when I helped someone or made a difference —people telling me how nice or kind I was.*

Being grateful has just become so much more natural with peace. I still have a gratitude journal, but I don't need to write it down so much, because it's in my heart, and I find myself saying "Thank You" all the time. The more I am grateful, the more comes to me because I know everything is being done in my best interest.

Lesson 135 of the Course says:

> *"What could you not accept, if you but knew that everything that happens, all events, past, present and to come, are gently planned by One Whose only purpose is your good? Perhaps you have misunderstood His plan, for He would never offer pain to you. But your defenses did not let you see His loving blessing shine in every step you ever took. While you made plans for death, He led you gently to eternal life."*

I **know** this is true – there is so much evidence in my life that I can't deny this truth, and I am completely grateful! As an example, I have always appreciated having a job, whether it was fun or not. I always looked for the good in each position I held, and sometimes the only good was that I was getting paid, but I stilled tried to be grateful. Today, I am the VP of Operations for a nonprofit, and I love my job – the work I do, the people I work with, and the satisfaction I feel when I leave the office each day. I am certain past gratitude has helped with my current peace with my career.

Through the Course, I learned that God doesn't want our gratitude but our trust, but we need to use gratitude to develop our appreciation of Him, which shows we trust Him. I wasn't sure I understood this concept until I applied it to my life and my giving. I always feel good when someone trusts me enough to just let me help; it could be as small as giving directions or sharing some advice that I think may be helpful with someone else. I think this is how God feels when we trust Him.

I have been fortunate to have many friends in my life, so friendships are another area where I have always been grateful, even for those that have been challenging. As I mentioned, I believe people come into our lives for a reason, so I always look for the purpose of my relationships and try to honor that purpose with each person. Most of my lasting friendships began during what I think is my spiritual growth season. These relationships provided encouragement and guidance, which helped keep me on my spiritual path.

Here are some stories that reflect how my friends helped me:

A friend once told me that she thought I "put people off," because I appeared "too nice." I am not a crier, but I broke down right there, because I was so upset. This really struck a nerve, so it had to be important. As I mentioned before, I never want to put people off, and I always try to be kind to everyone I meet, so she had to be wrong, and initially, I was mad at her. This bothered me for some time, so I started trying to figure out why. I came up with two reasons. The first seemed like she was trying to "fix" me. The Course says:

> "To the **ego,** it is kind and right and good to point out the errors and "correct" them."

So, knowing all this was from the ego, from fear, I wanted to learn what that fear meant. I learned and believed that we don't need to be fixed; we need to be loved, so her comment didn't make me feel loved and that hurt.

I also know if something hurts that bad on the outside, there's a deeper inner lesson to be learned. After I let my emotions go, and reflected further, I realized she made me feel like I was being a phony, and I think she was right in the sense that I was being a spiritual phony. People always tell me I am a great person, and I want to believe that, but I really don't. I try to be kind, considerate, compassionate, but the keyword is "try." It doesn't always come naturally to me, and I really wish it did. I would love to be like Mother Teresa, giving up everything to help those in need with complete humility, but that's just not me, and I always felt bad about that. Also, in the ego world, I know when I do something for someone, I am expecting something in return - acknowledgement, my own acceptance, and understanding, and this desire for some type of return also makes me feel guilty.

The funny thing is I was also embarrassed if I was acknowledged – what a mess, huh? I always thought I was a bad person because of these feelings, but the Course has shown me that as long as I am here, as long as I am an ego, these thoughts are going to occur, so I need to forgive myself for them, and give myself credit for trying. That is all that God asks of me, to try to remember Him, and let go of everything that happens here.

I am grateful to this friend for helping me with this lesson. I had grown from this experience to the point that when another friend had said I had a "gentle empathy and an ability to be present to other people, which is rare and comforting," I actually believed it a little, because I had let some of the guilt go, and empathy was becoming more natural for me. This was so nice to hear – I think empathy is what I need to offer my brothers, and I feel less resentful about it, so I think it is part of fulfilling my function.

While I love my friends and need to spend time with them, I am also grateful that I am never lonely when I am with myself. I spend a lot of time on my own, and the only time I feel like I need someone is when I want to go to dinner or have a glass of wine and chat with friends to catch up. I thought I needed a relationship to feel loved, but I realized I had one with God who loved me unconditionally, and that's enough.

Another gratitude is that children love me. I am not entirely sure why. I never wanted to be a mother, but I love kids, so I am grateful for the ones in my life that have made me feel special so many times. I think because I am not around them all of the time as a parent, it's easier for me to give them my undivided attention, which, like everyone, is what they really want. This also makes it easier for me to see more of their true self and accept them and respond to them as they are, because I don't see as much of their story, and they appreciate this, so we are joined in peace.

I hope sharing my lessons in this book is a right way of passing along my advice to those that need it, so I am also very grateful for this opportunity to share my happiness and peace with as many as possible in the hopes they experience the same feelings.

Journaling

As I noted above, I kept a gratitude journal for several years, but when I was very young, I was given a diary, and I have had some sort of journal ever since, so I have been writing my entire life. My journal entries include poems and thoughts I have written; entries from travel; and quotes, observations, insights, and messages I heard or read from other teachers through various books, songs, movies, and shows. I am sharing all of this information in this book, as I want to share my soul with the reader so I can grow towards the teacher I am trying to be.

I want to share my words, both written through my story and accumulated from other teachers on my path. I believe they are truths we all share that lead us to our common goal of peace. Our stories keep us separate, but our truths connect us, so in sharing, I hope to unite us all. Jesus said prayers are answered when two or more are joined in truth.

This project started several years ago when I decided I wanted to electronically record all of my diaries and journals. As I did this and was rereading my words, I realized universal truths were there, one kept building on another, so God had been guiding me all along. He is my author, so I turned my story over to Him to write. I am just borrowing His pen to pass along all I have learned, and I hope my book will be used as a sort of a consolidated spiritual handbook for the reader to add to their truths.

I suggest that everyone journal in some way, because by writing our thoughts down, we get them out of our head, where we can deal with them easier. We can review and analyze how our thoughts are serving us, and we can keep the ones that are giving us peace and eliminate the ones that cause fear.

Here is one of my poems related to my thoughts on peace –

CONNECTED

Look into the core,
We're all the same
Created as one
Under His name.
Connected in peace
Connected by love,
Here, now on earth,
Not just from above.
Forgiveness is needed,
Acceptance of others,

Connected to Him,
All one as brothers.
His love is equal for all,
He calls each to come,
The choice is ours,

To be separate or one.
Joined in peace,
Connected by love,
We have these in common,
He is enough.

Other words of advice or wisdom I heard and recorded on my path –

A Dayak Proverb says, "Where the heart is willing, it will find a thousand ways, but where it is unwilling it will find a thousand excuses."

For me, this meant - follow your heart. To do this, whenever I have a decision to make, I ask myself, "does this bring me peace?" If not, then I don't do it.

My parents always told me, "if you don't have anything nice to say, don't say anything."

While this can sometimes be a challenge in a defensive situation, I walk away before I say anything hurtful to alleviate the regret, I know I am going to have later.

No "should have, could have, would have." It is what it is! The only "should" is you should do whatever makes you happy with no regrets, no guilt, no worry, no fear, as long as it doesn't harm another.

All "problems" are solved in time because one problem has one solution. I am not separate from God. I just need to be patient, knowing that everything will be OK and that anything is possible with God.

Insanity is doing the same thing twice and expecting different results.

The Peace Network 9/21, *by Tom Carpenter speaks to how scale doesn't matter with regard to peace.*

"We frequently feel that if we expose in great detail how terrible things, such as the holocaust, have been, we will surely never allow them to occur again. History proves this is not the case. Holocausts, large and small, occur each time I judge myself, and my brother, as unworthy of being loved. Each time I want the stories we tell of hate and fear to be more real than risking relying on that loving peace we share with God, there is a cutting off in my mind of one that God created brother to me. What ends the need for holocausts is remembering that I am loved and expressing that in great detail by sharing the Presence of Love within me and everyone I meet!"

CONCLUSION

I WANTED TO SHARE ALL I HAVE learned using Joseph Campbell's Heroes Journey as a formula for the path I chose, because I feel it is true for each of us, and I want the reader to have a guide.

I love puzzles, and I see my life in this respect. All of the pieces from my journey - my travels, my setbacks that provided valuable lessons, and all of my teachers — guided me to my goal of peace, and in my own way, I became a teacher for those I am intended to guide. The pieces came together beautifully to complete my picture of peace, and with that, my goal has been realized. I am Pampered Peace Pilgrim, and it's ok, I don't have to feel guilty about wanting this for myself, because it makes me happy and brings me such peace, and I want to share that energy with everyone.

I realized all of my setbacks came from fear, and I was able to get to the heart of every problem by asking, "what am I afraid of?" My answer ultimately became "nothing," because my new logic was this - If I am OK now, at this moment, it is because everything that happened in the past is done, and all "problems" were solved. Knowing that I can have faith that any future "problem" will be solved, so I don't have to be afraid of anything, and I can be content that all will always be OK.

The Course told me the light has come – I have forgiven the world – I am healed and healer, peace and peacemaker, happy and happiness to all – I have the power right now to be entirely at peace and to offer it to everyone.

I am now willing to experience…

- Love
- Having more than enough money
- Forgetting my past and looking forward
- Not feeling guilty for anything
- Pride in myself and the things I do because I always try my best
- Expressing my true feelings
- Relying on myself for my own happiness
- Financial freedom

I am Pampered Peace Pilgrim – I travel a lot (sometimes in luxury), I move often (to nice apartments), I have many friends and people in my life to share my lessons, and now hopefully the readers of my book will find the peace I want to offer.

I hope by borrowing Peace's pen and continuing her message, I am honoring her journey and providing a guidebook for everyone to share with others so that their journeys are enhanced, they find the peace I have found and become the teachers they are destined to become.

I feel it is only appropriate to end with the most influential of Peace Pilgrim's advice – so simple and so true! It has guided me, and I hope it is useful to the reader. Enjoy your journey!

> *"Live in the present.*
> *Do the things you know need to be done.*
> *Do all the good you can each day.*
> *The future will unfold."*
> Peace Pilgrim

MORE TO SHARE

(Other Peace Pilgrims Showing Up on My Path)

I HAVE BEEN RECEIVING MESSAGES ALL MY life. Some were subtle, but as I wanted to find more peace, they became more evident and presented themselves more frequently through my favorite pastime of reading. I have already shared a lot, but all of the below had a great impact as well, so I want to include them also. I am only providing samples of each source, but all are worthy of experiencing in their entirety.

The Seven Spiritual Laws of Success, A Practical Guide to the Fulfillment of Your Dreams – **Deepak Chopra**

Advice is provided within each of the seven laws, so I try to apply this advice whenever I remember. Below are quick overviews.

Pure Potentiality

For me, this means to practice non-judgment. I need to see the potential in everyone, including myself.

Giving

I need to commit to keeping wealth circulating in my life by giving and receiving gifts of peace, caring, affection, appreciation, and love.

"Karma" or Cause and Effect

I need to witness the choices I make in each moment.

Whenever I make a choice, ask, "What are the consequences of this choice?" and "Will this choice bring fulfillment and happiness to me and also to those who are affected by this choice?"

Least Effort

Accept people, situations, circumstances, and events as they occur.

This means taking responsibility by not blaming anyone or anything for my situation. Know that every problem is an opportunity to ask for help from God, and He will answer, so no worry or effort is needed.

Don't be defensive – give up my need to defend my point of view. Remain open to all points of view. No opinion!

Intention and Desire

Give up attachment to outcome and focus on intention. What brings me peace.

Let the universe handle the details.

Detachment

Commit to detachment —allow myself and those around me to the freedom to be as they are.

Factor in uncertainty as an essential ingredient of my experience.

Get excited about all that can occur when I remain open to the infinity of choices.

"Dharma" or Purpose in Life

Seek my higher Self – awaken myself to the deep stillness within me.

Ask, "How can I serve?"

Dialogue on Awakening – Tom Carpenter

My Course mentor, Mrs. Lantos, introduced me to Tom Carpenter. He is a Course follower and teacher, and he has a way of expressing the theory of the Course in a way anyone can understand. In this book, he provides valuable guidance from Jesus, who he calls Brother. I am listing either quotes from Jesus (in *italics*), or my interpretation of his words, as they relate to Peace Pilgrim's mission and my life. He also has a Facebook page – The Peace Network – that I highly recommend following.

> *"Once the recognition of who you are becomes the reality in your conscious mind, you will discover the natural thing to do is simply to be it. This requires no effort."*

I sometimes think things are impossible or over-whelming, or that I have to work hard or struggle to have what I think I want, but in reality, if I have these thoughts, the truth is I am probably just not interested in what I am pursuing, because it isn't part of my nature – what comes naturally to me. I need to believe that all things in my best interest will occur effortlessly because they are coming from God, who truly knows what I need.

I wanted to know - how do I know when I'm being directed by my Higher Self? I was given the answer below:

"Listen to the voice that brings peace – it is the feeling of relaxing into something, the lack of the need to have a determination to overcome anything, that ultimately brings you into the recognition of that which you are seeking."

"Once you have made a commitment to do only those things that bring you peace, you will find peace in whatever you do."

"Be in a state that trusts and refuses to acknowledge fear, that accepts only that which brings you peace and sees Love beyond the façade of hate."

"So, if I do not anticipate problems with those around me as I choose to awaken, I will not have any?"

When we see daily activities as being chaotic or confusing, we should immediately know that this condition is reflective of our minds. The only way to change the situation is to change our minds. Our problem is our wrong thinking has been with us for so long; we think things are natural or "normal," so we think they are difficult to change.

"When you choose for peace and joy for both you and your brother, that will be the outcome regardless of circumstances."

For me, this is the Platinum Rule – do unto others as they would **have** you do unto them.

"Allow yourself to be in a state of joy and know that when you are in that state, you are in a state of God. The rest will happen."

When wondering if an answer has come from the Holy Spirit or me, I need to ask – "Have I become more loving? Have I become more peaceful? Do I find joy here?"

Pampered Peace Pilgrim directs my attention toward the memory of my Higher Self and does not promote fearful thinking – it gives me a sense of Love.

"As your mind lacks clarity, then those circumstances that you are manifesting in your physical world will equally lack clarity."

When peace is in my mind, when Love is in my mind, then that is what I will experience.

I Am Pampered Peace Pilgrim – Teacher of Peace

I don't need to think that I need to become something. I just have to be secure in knowing that the change is merely bringing me back into alignment with what I have always been. I need to think of it as a process of bringing myself out of amnesia.

The Course says there's one problem and one solution. The one problem is we think we are separate from God. The solution is we are not!

"The Truth doesn't change; only the vehicle which is necessary to accomplish your recognition of it will change."

We all have the same Truth (Love, Peace, Happiness) in us; we just all receive it differently on our journeys. Therefore, we need to seek our truth for ourselves and accept/allow others to find theirs in the best way.

I am the paint; I am the brush. But the creation of the canvas has already been done.

"You save the world by changing your vision to see it as it really is. You restore the world's sanity by reclaiming your right Mind, altering vision to see that which is reflective of the Mind of God."

If I am happy, living my truth, others will be happy - the Pampered Peace Pilgrim Partnership mission.

"When you become aware that all the planning and managing you have to do is to clearly align your focus on the feeling you wish to have from your experience, you will have defined the meaning it holds for you."

Trust my Self and I will find the safety and security I seek.

I am a pampered peace pilgrim, and that makes me happy, so God is happy to see me happy.

"The process of healing is one of letting go of all judgement and guilt which you have accumulated through past experiences."

Give up placing value on any type of limitation, and you will have a more evident recognition of how you truly are.

The story doesn't matter, but the feeling of happiness does, so we need to honor and accept whatever makes another happy. Accepting ideas, hobbies, talents, etc. = Love

As long as it doesn't cause harm – let it be.

Have no opinion – stay open to everything, everyone, every situation – knowing there could be another way of seeing them and just want Love and Peace.

"If peace is the basis for all things that exist in Reality, then how can you feel a connection with your Source unless you feel peace? What can peace be except a word unless you allow it to flow through you?"

I am the conduit for Love and Peace

God has given me the freedom to choose whatever I wish to see, and I must do the same for others.

I have always been Home, and my journey has just been used to expand my awareness, and if I just be, more and more will open, bringing more and more peace and Love.

There is nothing else to do.

Heal the World —

"And as you recognize that the source exists in a state of perfection, you have but to allow the expression of that perfection which is you, to acknowledge that this is so."

We need to deal with the cause — go to the source, which is God, and the expression of all Creation is you.

I am perfect, so I don't need to do anything.

Jesus' journey -" As he came to know the nature of his mind as part of the one Mind, he knew there was nothing he could not know. He also strongly felt that God had given him this revelation as an answer to his confusion, and found great comfort resting in the trust and peace of the Presence he now felt to be a part of him."

I felt this confusion also, and I think we all do in some form.

Jesus found duality, and once he did, he realized he couldn't reconcile the two worlds – truth and perception.

His revelation – truth must always point to oneness - perception will always separate.

God's answer to our duality is the Holy Spirit, as it is the means and end together. What to do and how to do it is always through the guidance of the Holy Spirit.

Jesus' revelation created a great shift in awareness.

"This beautifully loving teacher accessed a completely different, totally harmonious state of mind underlying the dualistic, conflicted ego perception. Never before had we realized there was an alternative to what we had perceived as truth. Not a way to change or purify what we had perceived, but what literally was a different way to perceive ourselves. And one that would deny all the body's eyes seemed to see. It was how and where God can be experienced."

Infinite Love has no definitions, no boundaries, or limitations.

Now, I make plans but then I give them to the Holy Spirit and stay open to whatever happens. It is my way of reconciling duality.

Change Your Thoughts – Change Your Life: Living the Wisdom of the Tao – Wayne Dyer

The Tao Te Ching (Tao) is a Chinese classic text written by sage Laozi that teaches philosophical and religious Taoism. The Tao is a Chinese word signifying "way" or "path," and it is an excellent resource to follow for a divine life, and Wayne Dyer does an amazing job of explaining how each verse applies to our everyday life.

I feel the overall theme of the Tao aligns with Peace's philosophy of "just be." It agrees that both internal peace/balance is needed for worldly peace/balance, and it is all about living in the middle.

Below, I am only providing my own very brief interpretation of what I feel are the relevant meanings that I have obtained from reading Wayne's book, A Course in Miracles, and the actual Tao by Laozi. For anyone on a spiritual journey and seeking peace, I recommend reading the Tao in some format.

- Let things unfold naturally without expectations – no "should be," but "just is," and that is OK. There will always be good/bad, wrong/right, so just accept what is without judgment or criticism – no opinion – find the middle or neutral ground.

- No one is special or better than anyone else. Criticism and judgment go away when we try to see ourselves in everyone.

- We need to know when to just stop, let go, and enjoy the fruits of our labor. Know when enough is enough.

- We need to go beyond sensory levels and live where inner convictions replace ego goals. We would also benefit from trusting our inner nature and stop believing others' opinions. Be guided by the "natural you" that comes from an independent mind. Trust yourself and stop pursuing approval.

- We need to live an Unhurried Life. The Course and the Bible say, "Be still and know that I am God," and have a mind willing to flow from this stillness.

- Change is the only constant – accept it.

- We need to see ourselves in harmony with rules, rather than because of them. Rules should come from a heart-based attitude, rather than rule-based thinking. We don't need rules when there is only a willingness to love and respect everyone and all things.

- The Tao provides everything we need, and we just need to be grateful.

- We need to trust in our own greatness. We came from greatness and from a purely natural source, so we must be great. Acknowledge this always. It is a sign of faith in our higher selves.

- Pay attention to the flow of your life, look for a joyous feeling, and follow it.

- We need to replace strong desires with calm contentment. When life is simple, pretenses fall away, and nature shines through. Because we come from God, we are naturally good, and nature is good without knowing it.

- There is no "them," only "us."

- Get out of the cycle of "striving and never arriving."

- Make compassion for all a personal philosophy.

- We can only do what we can do right now. Think small, rather than being overwhelmed by the big picture. Be in the now! No past to have regrets about and no worry of the future.

- Wayne Dyer says to copy the below words and put into practice, so I want to share!

Tao The Ching: A New Translation by Sam Hamill

"The sage does not hoard,

And thereby bestows.

The more he lives for others,

The greater his life.

The more he gives to others,

The greater his abundance."

The next three references also had an impact on my journey to peace, as sources that I still go back to again and again. The following is just a glimpse of some of the insights they provided me and align with the messages I shared throughout this book.

Three Magic Words – Uell S. Andersen

Through reading Wayne Dyer, this book was introduced to me. I won't make you wait to find out the Three Magic Words. They are, – "I AM GOD," which sounded arrogant to me, but I understand it now and hope the reader does as well. This book provides more support for The Course premise that God has never left us. It is also a source of excellent meditations.

"Yet inside you, a still small voice knows the truth, and no matter the strength of your rebellion away from your true self, the fact of your spiritual existence, the great I AM, will not be denied."

"...there is a power far greater than you and which you can use to make your life happy and fulfilled. The understanding of the power within yourself will expand your life to new and exciting horizons, will embark you upon the greatest adventure it is possible to know."

"Know that your every step is unerringly guided on a perfect route to your destination."

"Whatever has developed in our experience has not been brought to us by luck or fate or coincidence but is simply a physical manifestation of our thought and belief."

"The moment we say something is impossible, we make it impossible for God to manifest it through us."

Your Faith Is Your Fortune and *Awakened Imagination* - Neville Goddard

Reading books from Wayne Dyer also led me to Neville Goddard, who was a massive influence in connecting my Christian background with the Course, because he was able to take many of the biblical stories I had grown up with and explain them in their psychological terms, much in the same manner as the Course.

*I also think it's interesting that before I found his works, I had a Siamese cat (the love of my life) named Neville, who actually got his name from a cute Fig Newton commercial that always made me smile.

Neville noted that God Has given man only two gifts – mind and speech. Peace is found when the two are aligned. This is now my goal!

> *"When you can look upon man as one grand brotherhood without distinction of race or creed, then you will know that you have severe adhesions. With these ties cut, all that now separates you from your true being is your belief that you are man."*

> *"So, create a new heaven, enter into a new state of consciousness, and a new earth will appear."*

> *"Man discovers his awareness of being to be the inexhaustible treasure of the universe. In that day, when man makes this discovery, he dies as man and awakes as God."*

> *"'Father forgive them' is not the plea that comes once a year but the opportunity that comes every day."*

> *"To consciously create circumstances, man must consciously direct his inner speech, matching 'the still small voice' to his fulfilled desires."*

The Pilgrimage – Paulo Coelho

This work, and his most popular book, *The Alchemist*, should be read by anyone wanting to understand the journey of life.

> *"When you travel, you experience, in a very practical way, the act of rebirth. You confront completely new situations, the day passes more slowly, and on most journeys, you don't even understand the language the people speak. So, you are like a child just out of the womb."*

These words eloquently say how I feel about travel, and the below offer more powerful guidance for anyone.

"And most important, that you have to find support for yourself in the love that consumes during every minute of the climb because it is that love which directs and justifies your every step."

"And only when that happens — when you accept your role as a Master — will you learn all the answers you have in your heart."

"All at once, I felt exhausted by all that time spent on tests and battles and lessons and the pilgrimage."

"It is not a sin to be happy."

"He said that I should forget forever my unworthiness because the power had been reborn in me, in the same way that it could be reborn in all people who devote their lives to the good fight. A day would come — said the lamb's eye — when people would once again take pride in themselves, and then all of nature would praise the awakening of the God that had been sleeping within them."

YOUR JOURNEY

Now that I have shared my journey, I am providing the space below for you to document your path. I think it will provide an understanding of where you are and where you want to go. You may want to transfer this outline to your journal, so you can be as detailed as you think best.

Hero – You

Write down however you define or see yourself. What is your story? What do you tell others about yourself and what do you feel is true inside? Are there differences between the two stories? If so, see if you can reconcile the stories by applying your inner truth to your outer world. (Chapter Two)

CALL TO ADVENTURE

What are some of the moments, events, ideas, etc. that started you on your path? Find a quiet spot and focus on the things in your life that were important to you – defining moments that showed up as a deep desire for something more. (Chapter Three)

TEACHER(S)

What people, mentors, or ideologies impacted your journey? (Chapter Four)

SETBACKS

What are some of the roadblocks that crossed your path, taking you away from finding your goal? (Chapter Five)

GOAL

What are you trying to achieve? Again, give this some thought and try to be as specific as possible. (Chapter 6)

Hero becomes Teacher

How are you using your truth to impact others, improve lives (including your own), or being a positive role model? (Chapter Seven)

"STEPS TOWARD INNER PEACE"

- <u>Steps Toward Inner Peace</u> (From a KPFK radio talk, Los Angeles - 1964)

- <u>Summary</u>

    - <u>Four Preparations</u>
    - <u>Four Purifications</u>
    - <u>Four Relinquishments</u>

- <u>Thoughts</u>

- <u>From My Correspondence</u>

- <u>Peace Pilgrim's Progress</u> (Excerpts from the Newsletters)

This disCourse is lovingly dedicated to all seekers by Peace Pilgrim.

STEPS TOWARD INNER PEACE

IN MY EARLY LIFE I made two very important discoveries. In the first place I discovered that making money was easy. And in the second place I discovered that making money and spending it foolishly was completely meaningless. I knew that this was not what I was here for, but at that time (this was many years ago), I didn't know exactly what I *was* here for. It was out of a very deep seeking for a meaningful way of life, and after having walked all one night through the woods, that I came to what I now know to be a very important psychological hump. I felt a complete willingness, without any reservations, to give my life, to dedicate my life to service. I tell you, it is a point of no return. After that, you can never go back to completely self-centered living.

And so I went into the second phase of my life. I began to live to *give* what I could, instead of *get* what I could, and I entered a new and wonderful world. My life began to become meaningful. I attained the great blessing of good health; I haven't had a cold or headache since. (Most illness is psychologically induced.) From that time on, I have known that my life-work would be work for peace; that it would cover the entire peace picture - peace among nations, peace among groups, peace among individuals, and the very, very important inner peace. However, there's a great deal of difference between being willing to give your life, and actually giving your life, and for me, 15 years of preparation and of inner seeking lay between.

During this time I became acquainted with what Psychologists refer to as *Ego* and *Conscience*. I began to realize that it's as though we have two selves or two natures or two wills with two different viewpoints. Because the viewpoints were so different, I felt a struggle in my life at this period between the two selves with the two viewpoints. So there were hills and valleys - lots of hills and valleys. Then in the midst of the struggle there came a wonderful mountain-top experience, and for the first time I knew what inner peace was like. I felt a oneness - oneness with all my fellow human beings, oneness with all of creation. I have never felt really separate since. I could return again and again to this wonderful mountaintop, and then I could stay there for longer and longer periods of time, and just slip out occasionally. Then came a wonderful morning when I woke up and knew that I would never have to descend again into the valley. I knew that for me the struggle was over, that finally I had succeeded in giving my life, or finding inner peace. Again this is a point of no return. you can never go back into the struggle. The struggle is over now because you *will* do the right thing, and you don't need to be pushed into it.

However progress is not over. Great progress has taken place in this third phase of my life, but it's as though the central figure of the jigsaw puzzle of your life is complete and clear and unchanging, and around the edges other pieces keep fitting in. There is always a growing edge, but the progress is harmonious. There is a feeling of always being surrounded by all of the good things, like love and peace and joy. It seems like a protective surrounding, and there is an unshakeableness within which takes you through any situation you may need to face.

The world may look at you and believe that you are facing great problems, but always there are the inner resources to easily overcome these problems. Nothing seems difficult. There calmness and a serenity and unhurriedness - no more striving or straining about anything. Life is full and life is good, but life is nevermore overcrowded. That's a very important thing I've learned: If your life is in harmony with your part in the Life Pattern, and if you are obedient to the laws which govern this universe, then your life is full and good but not overcrowded. If it is overcrowded, you are doing more than is right for you to do, more than is your job to do in the total scheme of things.

Now there is a living to give instead of to get. As you concentrate on the giving, you discover that just as you cannot receive without giving, so neither can you give without receiving - even the most wonderful things like health and happiness and inner peace. There is a feeling of *endless energy* - it just never runs out; it seems to be as endless as air. You just seem to be plugged into the source of universal energy.

You are now in control of your life. You see, the ego is never in control. The ego is controlled by wishes for comfort and convenience on the part of the body, by demands of the mind, and by outbursts of the emotions. But the higher nature controls the body and the mind and the emotions. I can say to my body, "Lie down there on that cement floor and go to sleep," and it obeys. I can say to my mind, "Shut out everything else and concentrate on this job before you," and it's obedient. I can say to the emotions, "Be still, even in the face of this terrible situation," and they are still. It's a different way of living. The philosopher Thoreau wrote: *If a man does not keep pace with his companions, perhaps he hears a different drummer.* And now *you* are following a different drummer - the higher nature instead of the lower.

It was only at this time, in 1953, that I felt guided or called or motivated to begin my pilgrimage for peace in the world - a journey undertaken traditionally. The tradition of pilgrimage is a journey undertaken on foot and on faith, prayerfully and as an opportunity to contact people. I wear a lettered tunic in order to contact people. It says **'PEACE PILGRIM'** on the front. I feel that's my name now - it emphasizes my mission instead of me. And on the back it says **'25,000 MILES ON FOOT FOR PEACE.'** The purpose of the tunic is merely to make contacts for me. Constantly as I walk along the highways and through the cities, people approach me and I have a chance to talk with them about peace.

I have walked 25,000 miles as a penniless pilgrim. I own only what I wear and what I carry in my small pockets. I belong to no organization. I have said that I will walk until given shelter and fast until given food, remaining a wanderer until mankind has learned the way of peace. And I can truthfully tell you that without ever asking for anything, I have been supplied with everything needed for my journey, which shows you how *good* people really are.

With Me I carry always my peace message: *This is the way of peace: Overcome evil with good, falsehood with truth, and hatred with love.* There is nothing new about this message, except the practice of it. And the practice of it is required not only in the international situation but also in the personal situation. I believe that the situation in the world is a reflection of our own immaturity. If we were mature, harmonious people, war would be no problem whatever - it would be impossible.

All of us can work for peace. We can work right where we are, right within ourselves, because the more peace we have within our own lives, the more we can reflect into the outer situation. In faith, I believe that the wish to *survive* will push us into some kind of uneasy world peace which will then need to be supported by a great inner awakening if it is to endure. I believe we entered a new age when we discovered nuclear energy, and that this new age calls for a new renaissance to lift us to a higher level of understanding so that we will be able to cope with the problems of this new age. So, primarily my subject is peace within ourselves as a step toward peace in our world.

Now, when I talk about the steps toward inner peace, I talk about them in a framework, but there's nothing arbitrary about the number of steps. They can be expanded; they can be contracted. This is just a way of talking about the subject, but this is important: the steps toward inner peace are not taken in any certain order. The *first step* for one may be the *last step* for another. So, just take whatever steps seem easiest for you, and as you take a few steps, it will become easier for you to take a few more. In this area we really can share. None of you may feel guided to walk a pilgrimage, and I'm not trying to inspire you to walk a pilgrimage, but in the field of finding harmony in our own lives, we can share. And I suspect that when you hear me give some of the steps toward inner peace, you will recognize them as steps that you also have taken.

In the first place I would like to mention some preparations that were required of me. The first preparation is a *right attitude toward life*. This means - stop being an escapist! Stop being a surface-liver who stays right in the froth of the surface. There are millions of these people, and they never find anything really worthwhile. Be willing to face life squarely and get down beneath the surface of life where the verities and realities are to be found. That's what we are doing here now.

There's the whole matter of having a meaningful attitude for the problems that life may set before you. If only you could see the whole picture, if only you knew the whole story, you would realize that no problem ever comes to you that does not have a purpose in your life, that cannot contribute to your inner growth. When you perceive this, you will recognize problems as opportunities in disguise. If you did not face problems you would just drift through life, and you would not gain inner growth. It is through solving problems in accordance with the highest light that we have that inner growth is attained. Now, collective problems must be solved by us collectively, and no one finds inner peace who avoids doing his or her share in the solving of collective problems, like world disarmament and world peace. So let us always think about these problems together, talk about them together, and collectively work toward their solutions.

The second preparation has to do with *bringing our lives into harmony with the laws that govern this universe*. Created are not only the worlds and the beings but also the laws which govern them. Applying both in the physical realm and in the psychological realm, these laws govern human conduct. Insofar as we are able to understand and bring our lives into harmony with these laws, our lives will be in harmony. Insofar as we disobey these laws, we create difficulties for ourselves by our disobedience. We are our own worst enemies. If we are out of harmony through ignorance, we suffer somewhat; but if we *know better* and are still out of harmony, then we suffer a great deal. I recognize that these laws are well-known and well-believed, and therefore they just needed to be well-lived.

So I got busy on a very interesting project. This was *to live all the good things I believed in.* I did not confuse myself by trying to take them all at once, but rather, if I was doing something that I knew I should not be doing, I stopped doing it, and I always made a *quick relinquishment.* You see, that's the easy way. Tapering off is long and hard. And if I was not doing something that I knew I should be doing, I got busy on that. It took the living quite a while to catch up with the believing, but of course it can, and now if I believe something, I live it. Otherwise it would be perfectly meaningless. As I lived according to the highest light that I had, I discovered that other light was given, and that I opened myself to receiving more light as I lived the light I had.

These laws are the same for all of us, and these are the things that we can study and talk about together. But there is also a third preparation that has to do with something which is unique for every human life because every one of us has *a special place in the Life Pattern.* If you do not yet know clearly where you fit, I suggest that you try seeking it in receptive silence. I used to walk amid the beauties of nature, just receptive and silent, and wonderful insights would come to me. You begin to do your part in the Life Pattern by doing all the good things you feel motivated toward, even though they are just little good things at first. You give these priority in your life over all the superficial things that customarily clutter human lives.

There are those who know and do not do. This is very sad. I remember one day as I walked along the highway a very nice car stopped and the man said to me, "How wonderful that you are following your calling!" I replied, "I certainly think that everyone should be doing what feels right to do." He then began telling me what he felt motivated toward, and it was a good thing that needed doing. I got quite enthusiastic about it and took for granted that he was doing it. I said, "That's wonderful! How are you getting on with it?" And he answered, "Oh, I'm not doing it. That kind of work doesn't *pay* anything." And I shall never forget how desperately unhappy that man was. But you see, in this materialistic age we have such a false criterion by which to measure success. We measure it in terms of dollars, in terms of material things. But happiness and inner peace do not lie in that direction. If you know but do not do, you are a very unhappy person indeed.

There is also a fourth preparation, and it is the *simplification of life* to bring inner and outer well-being - psychological and material well-being - into harmony in your life. This was made very easy for me. Just after I dedicated my life to service, I felt that I could no longer accept *more* than I needed while others in the world have *less* than they need. This moved me to bring my life down to need-level. I thought it would be difficult. I thought it would entail a great many hardships, but I was quite wrong. Now that I own only what I wear and what I carry in my pockets, I don't feel deprived of anything. For me, what I want and what I need are exactly the same, and you couldn't give me anything I don't need.

I discovered this great truth: unnecessary possessions are just unnecessary burdens. Now I don't mean that all our needs are the same. Yours may be much greater than mine. For instance, if you have a family, you would need the stability of a family center for your children. But I do mean that anything beyond need - and need sometimes includes things beyond the physical needs, too - anything beyond need tends to become burdensome.

There is a great freedom in simplicity of living, and after I began to feel this, I found a harmony in my life between inner and outer well-being. Now there's a great deal to be said about such harmony, not only for an individual life but also for the life of a society. It's because as a world we have gotten ourselves so far out of harmony, so way off on the material side, that when we discover something like nuclear energy, we are still capable of putting it into a bomb and using it to kill people. This is because our inner well-being lags behind our outer well-being. The valid research for the future is on the *inner* side, on the psychological side, so that we will be able to bring these two into balance, so we will know how to use well the outer well-being we already have.

Then I discovered that there were some purifications required of me. The first one is such a simple thing: it is *purification of the body*. This has to do with your physical living habits. Do you eat sensibly, eating to live? I actually know people who live to eat. And do you know when to stop eating? That is a very important thing to know. Do you have sensible sleeping habits? I try to get to bed early and have plenty of hours of sleep. Do you get plenty of fresh air, sunshine, exercise and contact with nature? You'd think this might be the first area in which people would be willing to work, but from practical experience I've discovered it's often the last because it might mean getting rid of some of our bad habits, and there is nothing that we cling to more tenaciously.

The second purification I cannot stress too much because it is *purification of thought*. If you realized how powerful your thoughts are you would never think a negative thought. They can be a powerful influence for good when they're on the positive side, and they can and do make you physically ill when they're on the negative side.

I recall a man 65 years old when I knew him who manifested symptoms of what seemed a chronic physical illness. I talked with him and I realized that there was some bitterness in his life, although I could not find it at once. He got along well with his wife and his grown children, and he got along will in his community, but the bitterness was there just the same. I found that he was harboring bitterness against his long-dead father because his father had educated his brother and not him. As soon as he was able to relinquish this bitterness, the so-called chronic illness began to fade away, and soon it was gone.

If you're harboring the slightest bitterness toward anyone, or any unkind thoughts of any sort whatever, you must get rid of them quickly. They aren't hurting anyone but you. It is said that hate injures the hater, not the hated. It isn't enough just to do right things and say right things, you must also *think* right things before your life can come into harmony.

The third purification is *purification of desire.* What are the things you desire? Do you desire new clothing, or pleasures, or new household furnishings, or a new car? You can come to the point of oneness of desire just to know and do your part in the Life Pattern. When you think about it, is there anything else as really important to desire?

There is one more purification, and that is *purification of motive.* What is your motive for whatever you may be doing? If it is pure greed or self-seeking or the wish for self-glorification, I would say, *Don't do that thing.* Don't do anything you would do with such a motive. But it isn't that easy because we tend to do things with very mixed motives, good and bad motives all mixed together. Here's a man in the business world: his motives may not be the highest but mixed in with them are motives of caring for his family and perhaps doing some good in his community. Mixed motives!

Your motives, if you are to find inner peace, must be an outgoing motive - it must be service. It must be giving, not getting. I knew a man who was a good architect. It was obviously his right work, but he was doing it with the wrong motive. His motive was to make a lot of money and keep ahead of the Joneses. He worked himself into an illness, and it was shortly after, that I met him. I got him to do little things for service. I talked to him about the joy of service and I knew that after he had experienced this, he could never go back into really self-centered living. We corresponded a bit after that. On the third year of my pilgrimage route, I walked through his town and I hardly recognized him when I stopped in to see him. He was such a changed man! But he was still an architect. He was drawing a plan and he talked to me about it: "You see, I'm designing it this way to fit into their budget, and then I'll set it on their plot of ground to make it look nice." His motive was to be of service to the people that he drew plans for. He was a radiant and transformed person. His wife told me that his business had increased because people were now coming to him from miles around for home designs.

I've met a few people who had to change their jobs in order to change their lives, but I've met many more people who merely had to change their motive to service in order to change their lives.

Now, the last part. These are the relinquishments. Once you've made the first relinquishment, you have found inner peace because it's the *relinquishment of self-will*. You can work on this by refraining from doing any not-good thing you may be motivated toward, but you never suppress it! If you are motivated to do or say a mean thing, you can always think of a good thing. You deliberately turn around and use that *same energy* to do or say a good thing instead. It works!

The second relinquishment is *the relinquishment of the feeling of separateness*. We begin feeling very separate and judging everything as it relates to us, as though we were the center of the universe.

Even after we know better intellectually, we still judge things that way. In reality, of Course, we are all cells in the body of humanity. We are not separate from our fellow humans. The whole thing is a totality. It's only from that higher viewpoint that you can know what it is to love your neighbor as yourself. From that higher viewpoint there becomes just one realistic way to work, and that is for the good of the whole. As long as you work for your selfish little self, you're just one cell against all those other cells, and you're way out of harmony. But as soon as you begin working for the good of the whole, you find yourself in harmony with all of your fellow human beings. You see, it's the easy, harmonious way to live.

Then there is the third relinquishment, and that is *the relinquishment of all attachments.* Material things must be put into their proper place. They are there for use. It's all right to use them; that's what they're there for. But when they've outlived their usefulness, be ready to relinquish them and perhaps pass them on to someone who does need them. Anything that you cannot relinquish when it has outlived its usefulness possesses you, and in this materialistic age a great many of us are possessed by our possessions. We are not free.

There's another kind of possessiveness. *You do not possess any other human being,* no matter how closely related that other may be. No husband owns his wife; no wife owns her husband; no parents own their children. When we think we possess people there's a tendency to run their lives for them, out of this develops an extremely inharmonious situation. Only when we realize that we do not possess them, that they must live in accordance with their own inner motivations, do we stop trying to run their lives for them, and then we discover that we are able to live in harmony with them.

Now the last: *the relinquishment of all negative feelings*. I want to mention just one negative feeling which the nicest people still experience, and that negative feeling is *worry*. Worry is not *concern* which would motivate you to do everything possible in a situation. Worry is a useless mulling over of things we cannot change. Let me mention just one technique. Seldom do you worry about the present moment; it's usually all right. If you worry, you agonize over the past which you should have forgotten long ago, or you're apprehensive over the future which hasn't even come yet. We tend to skim right over the present time. Since this is the only moment that one can live, if you don't live it you never really get around to living at all. If you do live this present moment, you tend not to worry. For me, every moment is a new opportunity to be of service.

One last comment about negative feelings which helped me very much at one time and has helped others. No outward thing - nothing, nobody from without - can hurt me inside, psychologically. I recognized that I could only be hurt psychologically by my own wrong actions, which I have control over; by my own wrong reactions - they are tricky, but I have control over them, too; or by my own inaction in some situations, like the present world situation, that needs actions from me. When I recognized all this, how free I felt! And I just stopped hurting myself. Now someone could do the meanest thing to me and I would feel deep compassion for this out-of-harmony person, this psychologically sick person who is capable of doing mean things. I certainly would not hurt myself by a wrong reaction of bitterness or anger. You have complete control over whether or not you will be hurt psychologically, and any time you want to, you can stop hurting yourself.

These are the steps toward inner peace that I wanted to share with you. There's nothing new about this. This is universal truth. I merely talked about these things in my own everyday words in terms of my own personal experience with them. The laws which govern this universe work for good as soon as we obey them, and anything contrary to these laws doesn't last long. It contains within itself the seeds of its own destruction. The good in every human life always makes it possible for us to obey these laws. We do have free will about all this, and therefore how soon we obey and thereby find harmony, both within ourselves and within our world, is up to us.

(From a KPFK radio talk, Los Angeles)

SUMMARY

FOUR PREPARATIONS

1. Assume right attitude toward life

Stop being an escapist or a surface-liver as these attitudes can only cause in harmony in your life. Face life squarely and get down below the froth on its surface to discover its verities and realities. Solve the problems that life sets before you, and you will find that solving them contributes to your inner growth. Helping to solve collective problems contributes also to your growth, and these problems should never be avoided.

2. Live good beliefs.

The laws governing human conduct apply as rigidly as the law of gravity. Obedience to these laws pushes us toward harmony; disobedience pushes us toward in harmony. Since many of these laws are already common belief, you can begin by putting into practice all the good things you believe. No life can be in harmony unless belief and practice are in harmony.

3. Find your place in the Life Pattern.

You have a part in the scheme of things. What that part is you can know only from within yourself. You can seek it in receptive silence. You can begin to live in accordance with it by doing all the good things you are motivated toward and giving these things priority in your life over all the superficial things that customarily occupy human lives.

4. Simplify life to bring inner and outer well-being into harmony.

Unnecessary possessions are unnecessary burdens. Many lives are cluttered not only with unnecessary possessions but also with meaningless activities. Cluttered lives are out-of-harmony lives and require simplification. Wants and needs can become the same in a human life and, when this is accomplished, there will be a sense of harmony between inner and outer well-being. Such harmony is needful not only in the individual life but in the collective life too.

FOUR PURIFICATIONS

1. Purification of the bodily temple.

Are you free from all bad habits? In your diet do you stress the vital foods - the fruits, whole grains, vegetables and nuts? Do you get to bed early and get enough sleep? Do you get plenty of fresh air, sunshine, exercise, and contact with nature? If you can answer "Yes" to all of these questions, you have gone a long way toward purification of the bodily temple.

2. Purification of the thoughts.

It is not enough to do right things and say right things. You must also *think* right things. Positive thoughts can be powerful influences for good. Negative thoughts can make you physically ill. Be sure there is no unpeaceful situation between yourself and any other human being, for only when you have ceased to harbor unkind thoughts can you attain inner harmony.

3. Purification of the desires.

Since you are here to get yourself into harmony with the laws that govern human conduct and with your part in the scheme of things, your desires should be focused in this direction.

4. Purification of motives.

Obviously, your motive should never be greed or self-seeking, or the wish for self-glorification, you shouldn't even have the selfish motive of attaining inner peace for yourself. To be of service to your fellow humans must be your motive before your life can come into harmony.

FOUR RELINQUISHMENTS

1. Relinquishment of self-will.

You have, or it's as though you have, *two selves:* the lower self that usually governs you selfishly, and the higher self which stands ready to use you gloriously. You must subordinate the lower self by refraining from doing the not-good things you are motivated toward, not suppressing them but transforming them so that the higher self can take over your life.

2. Relinquishment of the feeling of separateness.

All of us, all over the world, are cells in the body of humanity. You are not separate from your fellow humans, and you cannot find harmony for yourself alone. You can only find harmony when you realize the oneness of all and work for the good of all.

3. Relinquishment of attachments.

Only when you have relinquished all attachments can you be really free. Material things are here for use, and anything you cannot relinquish when it has outlived its usefulness possesses you. You can only live in harmony with your fellow humans if you have no feeling that you possess them, and therefore do not try to run their lives.

4. Relinquishment of all negative feelings.

Work on relinquishing negative feelings. If you live in the present moment, which is really the only moment you have to live, you will be less apt to worry. If you realize that those who do mean things are psychologically ill, your feelings of anger will turn to feelings of pity. If you recognize that all of your inner hurts are caused by your own wrong actions or your own wrong reactions or your own wrong inaction, then you will stop hurting yourself.

THOUGHTS

* WE CAN ALL SPEND OUR LIVES going about doing good. Every time you meet a person, think of some encouraging thing to say - a kind word, a helpful suggestion, an expression of admiration. Every time you come into a situation, think of some good thing to bring - a thoughtful gift, a considerate attitude, a helping hand.

* There is a criterion by which you can judge whether the thoughts you are thinking and the things you are doing are right for you. That criterion is, *Have they brought you inner peace?* If they have not, there is something wrong with them - so keep trying.

*If you love people enough, they will respond lovingly. If I offend people, I blame myself, for I know that if my conduct had been correct, they would not have been offended, even though they did not agree with me. "Before the tongue can speak, it must have lost the power to wound."

*To those who feel depressed, I would say: Try keeping your surroundings full of beautiful music and lovely flowers. Try reading and memorizing thoughts that inspire. Try making a list of all the things you have to be thankful for. If there is some good thing that you have always wanted to do, start doing it. Make a meaningful schedule for yourself and keep to that schedule.

*Although others may feel sorry for you, *never* feel sorry for yourself - it has a deadly effect on spiritual well-being. Recognize all problems, no matter how difficult, as opportunities for spiritual growth, and make the most of these opportunities.

*From all the things you read and from all the people you meet, take what is good - what you own 'Inner Teacher' tells you is for you - and leave the rest. For guidance and for truth, it is much better to look to the Source through your own 'Inner Teacher' than to look to people or books. Books and people can merely inspire you. Unless they awaken something within you, nothing worthwhile has been accomplished.

*No one is truly free who is still attached to material things, or to places, or to people. We must be able to use things when we need them and then relinquish them without regret when they have outlived their usefulness. We must be able to appreciate and enjoy the places where we tarry, and yet pass on without anguish when we are called elsewhere. We must be able to live in loving association with people without feeling that we possess them and must run their lives. Anything that you strive to hold captive will hold you captive, and if you desire freedom you must give freedom.

*The spiritual life is the real life - all else is illusion and deception. Only those who are attached to God alone are truly free.

Only those who live up to the highest light they have find their lives in harmony. Those who act on their highest motivations become a power for good. It is not important that others be noticeably affected. Results should never be sought or desired. Know that every right thing you do - every good thing you say - every positive thought you think- has good effect.

*All people can be peace workers. Whenever you bring harmony into any unpeaceful situation, you contribute to the total peace picture. Insofar as you have peace in your own life, you reflect it into your surroundings and into the world.

*That which is received from without can be compared with knowledge. It leads to a believing, which is seldom strong enough to motivate to action. That which is confirmed *from within* after it is contacted from without, or that which is directly perceived *from within* (which is my way), can be compared with wisdom. It leads to a *knowing,* and action goes right along with it.

*In our spiritual development we are often required to pull up roots many times and to close many chapters in our lives until we are no longer attached to any material thing and can love all people without any attachment to them.

*You cannot leave a situation without spiritual injury unless you leave it lovingly.

*If you want to teach people, young or old, you must start where they are - at their level of understanding. If you see that they are already beyond your level of understanding, let them teach you.

Since steps toward spiritual advancement are taken in such varied order, most of us can teach one another.

*Physical violence can end even before we have learned the way of love, but psychological violence will continue until we do. Only outer peace can be had through law. The way to inner peace is through love.

*Concentrate on giving so that you may open yourself to receiving. Concentrate on living according to the light you have, so that you may open yourself to more light.

*Sometimes difficulties of the body come to show that the body is just a transient garment - that the reality is the indestructible essence which activates the body.

*After you have found inner peace, spiritual growth takes place harmoniously because you - now governed by the higher self - will to do God's will and do not need to be pushed into it.

*Nothing threatens those who do God's will, and God's will is love and faith. Those who feel hate and fear are out of harmony with God's will and are likely to have difficulties.

*All difficulties in your life have a purpose. They are pushing you toward harmony with God's will.

*There is *always* a way to do right!

*What we suffer from is *immaturity*. If we were mature people, war would be no problem - it would be impossible.

*Of Course, I trust the Law of Love! Since the universe operates in accordance with the Law of Love, how could I trust anything else?

*For Light I go directly to the Source of Light, not to any of the reflections. Also, I make it possible for more Light to come to me by living up to the highest Light I have. You cannot mistake Light coming from the Source, for it comes with *complete understanding* so that you can explain and discuss it.

*Judging others will avail you nothing and injure you spiritually. Only if you can inspire others to judge themselves will anything worthwhile have been accomplished.

*Never think of any right effort as being fruitless - *all* right effort bears good fruit, whether we see results or not. Just concentrate on thinking and living and acting for peace, and inspiring others to do likewise, leaving results in God's hands.

*You cannot change anyone except yourself. After you have become an example, you can inspire others to change themselves.

*In a conflict situation you must be thinking of a solution which is fair to all concerned, instead of a solution which is of advantage to you. Only a solution which is fair to all concerned can be workable in the long run.

*Your motives must be good if your work is to have a good effect.

FROM MY CORRESPONDENCE

Q: *Do you work for a living?*
A: I work for my living in an unusual way. I give what I can through thoughts and words and deeds to those whose lives I touch and to humanity. In return I accept what people want to give, but I do not ask. They are blessed by their giving and I am blessed by my giving.

Q: *Why don't you accept money?*
A: Because I talk about spiritual truth, and spiritual truth should never be sold - those who sell it injure themselves spiritually. The money that comes in the mail - without being solicited - I do not use for myself; I use it for printing and postage. Those who attempt to buy spiritual truth are trying to get it before they are ready. In this wonderfully well-ordered universe, when they are ready, it will be given.

Q: *Don't you get lonely or discouraged or tired?*
A: No. When you live in constant communication with God, you cannot be lonely. When you perceive the working of God's

wonderful plan and know that all good effort bears good fruit, you cannot be discouraged. When you have found inner peace, you are in contact with the source of universal energy and you cannot be tired.

Q: *What can retirement mean to a person?*
A: Retirement should mean, not a cessation of activity, but a change of activity with a more complete giving of your life to service. It should therefore be the most wonderful time of your life - the time when you are happily and meaningfully busy.

Q: *How can I feel close to God?*
A: God is Love, and whenever you reach out in loving kindness, you are expressing God. God is Truth, and whenever you seek truth, you are seeking God. God is Beauty, and whenever you touch the beauty of a flower or a sunset, you are touching God. God is the Intelligence that creates all and sustains all and binds all together and gives life to all. Yes, God is the Essence of all. So you are within God and God is within you - you could not be where God is not. Permeating all is the law of God - physical law and spiritual law. Disobey it and you feel unhappiness - you feel separated from God. Obey it and you feel harmony - you feel close to God.

Q: *What are the good things, and how do I fill my life with them?*
A: Good things are of benefit to you and to others. You may get some inspiration from the outside, but in the final analysis you must know from the inside what good things you want to fill your life with. Then you can make a schedule of what you think the good life should be like, and live according to that schedule.

It may include something beneficial to the body - like walking or exercise. Or something stimulating to the intellect - like meaningful reading. And something uplifting for the emotions - like good music. But most important of all, it needs to include service to others if it is to be spiritually beneficial to you.

Q: *When confronted with a problem, can I do anything about it intellectually?*
A: If it's a health problem, ask yourself, "Have I abused my body?" If it's a psychological problem, ask yourself, "Have I been as loving as God would want me to be?" If it's a financial problem, ask yourself, "Have I lived within my means?" What you do in the present creates the future, so use the present to create a wonderful future. Constantly through thought you are creating your inner conditions and helping to create the conditions around you. So keep your thoughts on the positive side, think about the best that could happen, think about the good things you want to happen - think about God!

Q: *How can I begin to really live life?*
A: I began to really live life when I began to look at every situation and think about how I could be of service in that situation. I learned that I should not be pushy about helping, but just willing. Often I could give a helping hand - or perhaps a loving smile or a word of cheer. I learned it is through giving that we receive the worthwhile things of life.

Q: *How does an ordinary housewife and mother find what you seem to possess?*
A: One who is in the family pattern (as most people are) finds inner peace in the same way that I found it. Obey God's laws,

which are the same for all of us - not only the physical laws, but also the spiritual laws which govern human conduct. You might start by living all the good things you believe, as I did. Find and fit into your special place in the divine plan, which is unique for every human soul. You might try seeking in receptive silence, as I did. Being in the family pattern is not a block to spiritual growth, and in some ways it is an advantage. We grow through problem-solving, and being in the family pattern provides plenty of problems to grow on. When we enter the family pattern, we have our first outgoingness from self-centeredness to family centeredness. Pure love is a willingness to give without a thought of receiving anything in return, and the family pattern provides the first experience of pure love - a mother's and father's love for their baby.

Q: *Will there always be pain in one's becoming more beautiful?*
A: There will be pain in your spiritual growth until you will to do God's will and no longer need to be pushed into it. When you are out of harmony with God's will, problems come - their purpose is to push you into harmony. If you would willingly do God's will, you could avoid the problems.

Q: *Will I ever come into a state of feeling at rest, with no more need to become?*
A: When you have found inner peace, you have no more feeling of the need to become - you are content to be, which includes following your divine guidance. However, you keep on growing - but harmoniously.

Q: *What is a truly religious person?*
A: I would say that a truly religious person has religious attitudes: a loving attitude toward fellow human beings, an obedient attitude toward God - toward God's laws and God's guidance, and a religious attitude toward self - knowing that you are more than the self-centered nature, more than the body, and life is more than the earth life.

Q: *What overcomes fear?*
A: I would say that religious attitudes overcome fear. If you have a loving attitude toward your fellow human beings, you will not fear them. *"Perfect love casteth out fear."* An obedient attitude toward God will bring you into constant awareness of God's presence, and then fear is gone. When you know that you are only wearing the body, which can be destroyed - that you are the reality which activates the body and cannot be destroyed - how can you be afraid?

PEACE PILGRIM'S PROGRESS

FOUR LETTERS: One day as I was answering my mail a woman said to me, "What can people do for peace?" I replied, "Let's see what these letters say." The first one said, "I'm a farm housewife. Since talking with you, I've realized I should be doing something for peace - especially since I'm raising four sons. Now I am writing one letter every day to someone in our government or in the United Nations who has done something for peace, commending them to give them moral support." The next one said, "World peace seemed a bit too big for me, but since talking with you, I have joined the Human Relations Council in my town, and I'm working on peace among groups." The third one said, "Since talking with you I have resolved an unpeaceful situation between myself and my sister-in-law." The last one said, "Since talking with you, I have cut out smoking." When you do something for world peace, peace among groups, peace among individuals, or your own inner peace, *you improve the total peace picture.* Whenever you bring harmony into any unpeaceful situation, you contribute to the cause of peace.

the MOST VALUABLE THINGS: After a wonderful sojourn in the wilderness, I walked again alone the streets of a city which was my home awhile. It is 1:00 p.m. Hundreds of neatly-dressed human beings with pale or painted faces are hurrying in rather orderly lines to and from their places of employment. I, in my faded shirt and well-worn slacks, walk among them. The rubber soles of my soft canvas shoes move noiselessly along beside the clatter of trim, tight shoes with high heels. In the poorer sections I am tolerated. In the wealthier sections some glances seem a bit startled, and some are disdainful. On both sides of us as we walk are displayed the things which we can buy if we are willing to stay in the orderly lines, day after day, year after year. Some of the things are more or less useful, many are utter trash - some have a claim to beauty, many are garishly ugly. Thousands of things are displayed - and yet the most valuable things are missing. Freedom is not displayed, nor health, nor happiness, nor peace of mind. To obtain these, my friends, you too may need to escape from the orderly lines and risk being looked upon disdainfully.

NEGATIVE *vs.* POSITIVE: I have chosen the positive approach - instead of stressing the bad things which I am against, I stress the good things which I am for. Those who choose the negative approach dwell on what is wrong, resorting to judgement and criticism, and sometimes even to name-calling. Naturally, the negative approach has a detrimental effect on the person who uses it, while the positive approach has a good effect. When evil is attacked, it mobilizes, although it may have been weak and unorganized before, and therefore the attack gives it validity and strength. When there is no attack, but instead good influences are brought to bear upon the situation, not only does the evil tend to fade away, but the evil-doer tends to be transformed. The positive approach inspires - the negative approach makes angry. When you make people angry they act in accordance with their baser instincts, often violently and irrationally. When you inspire people, they act in accordance with their higher instincts, sensibly and rationally. Anger is transient, whereas inspiration sometimes has a lifelong effect.

WORKING FOR PEACE: A few really dedicated people can offset the ill effects of masses of out-of-harmony people, so we who work for peace must not falter, we must continue to pray for peace and to act for peace in whatever way we can. We must continue to speak for peace and to live the way of peace; to inspire others, we must continue to think of peace and to know it is possible. What we dwell upon we help to bring into manifestation. One little person, giving all of her time to peace, makes news. Many people, giving some of their time, can make history.

BLESSED are they who give without expecting even thanks in return, for they shall be abundantly rewarded.

BLESSED are they who translate every good thing they know into action - even higher truths shall be revealed to them.

BLESSED are they who do God's will without asking to see results, for great shall be their recompense.

BLESSED are they who love and trust their fellow human beings, for they shall reach the good in people and receive a loving response.

BLESSED are they who have seen reality, for they know that not the garment of clay but that which activates the garment of clay is real and indestructible.

BLESSED are they who see the change we call death as a liberation from the limitations of this earth-life, for they shall rejoice with their loved ones who make the glorious transition.

BLESSED are they who after dedicating their lives and thereby receiving a blessing have the courage and faith to surmount the difficulties of the path ahead, for they shall receive a second blessing.

BLESSED are they who advance toward the spiritual path without the selfish motive of seeking inner peace, for they shall find it.

BLESSED are those who instead of trying to batter down the gates of the kingdom of heaven approach them humbly and lovingly and purified, for they shall pass right through.

YOU CAN KNOW GOD: There is a power greater than ourselves which manifests itself within us as well as everywhere else in the universe. This I call God. Do you know what it is to know God - to have God's constant guidance - a constant awareness of God's presence? To know God is to reflect love toward all people and all creations. To know God is to feel peace within - a calmness, a serenity, an unshakeableness which enables you to face any situation. To know God is to be so filled with joy that it bubbles over and goes forth to bless the world. I have only one desire now - to do God's will for me - there is no conflict. When God guides me to walk a pilgrimage I do it gladly. When God guides me to do other things I do them just as gladly. If what I do brings criticism upon me I take it with head unbowed. If what I do brings me praise, I pass it immediately along to God, for I am only the little instrument through which God does the work. When God guides me to do something I am given strength, I am given supply, I am shown the way, I am given the words to speak. Whether the path is easy or hard I walk in the light of God's love and peace and joy, and I turn to God with psalms of thanksgiving and praise. This it is to know God. And knowing God is not reserved for the great ones. It is for little folks like you and me. God is always seeking you - every one of you. You can find God if you will only seek - by obeying divine laws, by loving people, by relinquishing self-will, attachments, negative thoughts and feelings. And when you find God it will be in the stillness. You will find God within.

ON FEAR: There's no greater block to world peace or inner peace than fear. What we fear we tend to develop an unreasoning hatred for, so we come to hate and fear. This not only injures us psychologically and aggravates world tension, but through such negative concentration we tend to attract the things we fear. If we fear nothing and radiate love, we can expect good things to come. How much this world needs the message and example of love and faith!

the FREEDOM OF SIMPLICITY: Some seem to think my life dedicated to simplicity and service is austere and joyless, but these do not know the freedom of simplicity. I know enough about food to nourish my body properly, and I have excellent health. I enjoy food, but I eat to live. I do not live to eat, and I know when to stop eating. I am not enslaved by food. My clothes are most comfortable as well as most practical. My shoes, for instance, have soft fabric tops and soft rubberlike soles - I feel free as though I were walking barefoot. I am not enslaved by fashion. I am not a slave to comfort and convenience - for instance, I sleep equally well in a soft bed or on the grass beside the road. I am not burdened by unnecessary possessions or meaningless activities. My life is full and good, but not overcrowded, and I do my work easily and joyously. I feel beauty all around me and I see beauty in everyone I meet - for I see God in everything. I recognize the laws which govern this universe, and I find harmony through gladly and joyously obeying them. I recognize my part in the Life Pattern, and I find harmony through gladly and joyously living it. I recognize my oneness with all mankind and my oneness with God. My happiness overflows in loving and giving toward everyone and everything.

ON PEOPLE IN OUR TIMES: In order to help usher in the golden age, we must see the good in people - we must know that it is there, no matter how deeply it may be buried. Yes, apathy is there and selfishness is there - but good is there also. It is not through judgement that the good can be reached, but through love and faith. Love can save the world from nuclear destruction. Love God - turn to God with receptiveness and responsiveness. Love your fellow human beings - turn to them with friendliness and givingness. Make yourself fit to be called a child of God by living the Way of Love!

SPIRITUAL GROWTH is a process the same as physical growth or mental growth. Five year old children do not expect to be as tall as their parents at their next birthday; the first grader does not expect to graduate into college at the end of the term; the truth student should not expect to attain inner peace overnight.

MAGIC FORMULAS: There is a magic formula for resolving conflicts. It is this: *Have as your objective the resolving of the conflict, not the gaining of advantage.* There is a magic formula for avoiding conflicts. It is this: *Be concerned that you do not offend, not that you are not offended.*

ON IMMATURITY: What people really suffer from is immaturity. Among mature people war would not be a problem - it would be impossible. In their immaturity people want, at the same time, peace and the things which make war. However, people can mature just as children grow up. Yes, our institutions and our leaders reflect our immaturity, but as we mature we will elect better leaders and set up better institutions. It always comes back to the thing so many of us wish to avoid - working to improve ourselves.

MY MESSAGE: My friends, the world situation is grave. Humanity with fearful faltering steps, walks a knife-edge between complete chaos and a golden age, while strong forces push toward chaos. Unless we, the people of the world, awake from our lethargy and push firmly and quickly away from chaos, all that we cherish will be destroyed in the holocaust which will descend.

This is the way of peace: Overcome evil with good, falsehood with truth, and hatred with love.

The Golden Rule would do as well. Please don't say lightly that these are just religious concepts and not practical. These are laws governing human conduct, which apply as rigidly as the law of gravity. When we disregard these laws in any walk of life, chaos results. Through obedience to these laws this frightened, war-weary world of ours could enter into a period of peace and richness beyond our fondest dreams.

GRASS-ROOTS PEACE ACTIVITY: You can start a Community Peace Fellowship with a peace prayer group for seeking the way of peace. In some places my literature has been used since it deals with peace from a spiritual standpoint. Read a paragraph, dwell upon it in receptive silence, then talk about it. Anyone who can understand and feel the spiritual truths contained therein is spiritually ready to work for peace.

Then would come a Peace Study Group. We need to get a clear picture of what the present world situation is like and what will be needed to convert it into a peaceful world situation. Certainly all present wars must cease. Obviously, we need to find a way to lay down our arms together. We need to set up mechanisms to avoid physical violence in a world where psychological violence still exists. *All* nations need to give up one right to the United Nations - the right to make war.

We people of the world need to learn to put the welfare of the whole human family above the welfare of any group. Starvation and suffering need to be alleviated, as do fear and hatred. There are some national problems in connection with peace. Work needs to be done on peace among groups. Our number one national problem is the adjustment of our economy to a peacetime situation. We need a Peace Department in our national government to do extensive research on peaceful ways of resolving conflicts. Then we can ask other countries to create similar departments.

After world problems and steps toward their solutions become pretty clear to you, you are ready to become a Peace Action group. You can become a Peace Action group gradually - acting upon any problem that you have learned to understand. Peace action should always take the form of living the way of peace. It can also take the form of letter-writing - to commend those who have done something good for peace, to members of Congress about peace legislation, to editors on peace subjects, to friends on what you have learned about peace. It can take the form of public meetings on peace subjects, speakers on peace subjects, distributing peace literature, talking to people about peace, a Peace Week, A Peace Fair, a Peace Walk, or a Peace Float. It can take the form of voting for those who are committed to the way of peace.

Grass-roots peace work is vitally important. In this crisis period, there should be a Community Peace Fellowship in every town. Such a group can begin with a handful of concerned people. It can begin with you!

REFERENCES

A Course in Miracles. Second and Third Editions, 1992 and 2007, respectively, published by the Foundation for Inner Peace, PO Box 598, Mill Valley, CA USA 94942.

Peace Pilgrim, Her Life and Work in Her Own Words. Santa Fe, New Mexico Copyright 1982, 1991 by Friends of Peace Pilgrim.

Anderson, Uell. *Three Magic Words.* First Paperback Edition

Carpenter, Tom. 2012. *Dialogue on Awakening, Communion with a Loving Brother.* Copyright 2012 by Linda and Tom Carpenter.

Chopra, Deepak. 1994. *The Seven Spiritual Laws of Success, A Practical Guide to the Fulfillment of Your Dreams. Novato, CA.* Copyright 1994 by New World Library.

Coehlo, Paulo. 1987. *The Pilgrimage.* New York. Copyright 1987 by Paulo Coehlo.

Dyer, Wayne.2007. *Change Your Thoughts-Change Your Life, Living the Wisdom of the Tao.* Copyright 2007 by Wayne Dyer.

Goddard, Neville. 2011. *Your Faith is Your Fortune.* Blacksburg, Virginia. Copyright 2011 by Wilder Publications.

Neville.2010 7th Printing. *Awakened Imagination.* Camarillo, California. Copyright 1946 by Neville.

Singer, Michael. *The Untethered Soul, the journey beyond yourself.* Oakland, California. Copyright 2007 by Michael Singer and New Harbinger Publications, Inc.

Williamson, Marianne. 2012. *The Law of Devine Compensation, On Work, Money and Miracles.* Copyright 2012 by Marianne Williamson.